NOSTRADAMUS

NOSTRADAMUS
THE PROPHECIES

J. ANDERSON BLACK

GREENWICH EDITIONS

This edition published in 1998 by
Greenwich Editions, Blenheim Court, London N7 9NT

Published by Blitz Editions
an imprint of Bookmart Ltd
Registered Number 2372865
Trading as Bookmart Ltd
Desford Road
Enderby
Leicester LE9 5AD

This book created by Amazon Publishing Ltd, Middlesex
Editor: Ray Granger
Design: wilson design associates

Printed and bound in Great Britain by
The Guernsey Press Co. Ltd., Guernsey, Channel Islands

ISBN 0-86288-215-X

NOSTRADAMUS
THE MAN AND
PHYSICIAN

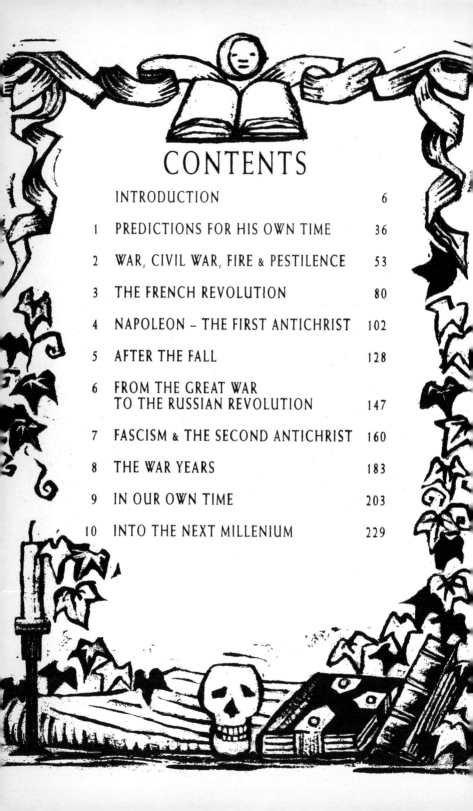

CONTENTS

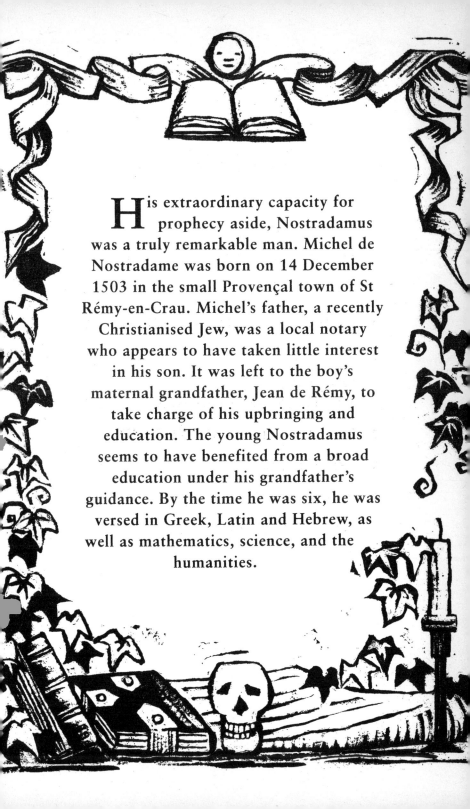

His extraordinary capacity for prophecy aside, Nostradamus was a truly remarkable man. Michel de Nostradame was born on 14 December 1503 in the small Provençal town of St Rémy-en-Crau. Michel's father, a recently Christianised Jew, was a local notary who appears to have taken little interest in his son. It was left to the boy's maternal grandfather, Jean de Rémy, to take charge of his upbringing and education. The young Nostradamus seems to have benefited from a broad education under his grandfather's guidance. By the time he was six, he was versed in Greek, Latin and Hebrew, as well as mathematics, science, and the humanities.

Jean de Rémy, a doctor by profession, had served as personal physician to the royal house of Provence, and he encouraged his ward to assist him in the gathering of herbs and the preparation of medicines. Though Nostradamus never refers to it in his own writing, it is almost certain that his grandfather also instructed him in astrology, magic and alchemy, as all these subjects were inextricably linked with medicine in the fifteenth and sixteenth centuries. However, with the Inquisition in full swing, it was not prudent to flaunt such learning. Nostradamus was only eight when Jean de Rémy died, and he returned home to his parents. There, his education was taken over by his other grandfather, Pierre de Nostradame. Michel was a brilliant scholar and, at the age of 14, he was considered to be ready to enter the university at Avignon.

Michel's first task was to satisfy the university examiners that he was indeed a suitable pupil. He was given oral examinations in grammar, rhetoric and philosophy. The first two subjects seem to have caused him little trouble. Most mediaeval scholarship was a matter of reciting prepared texts and his memory was astonishingly good. Where he genuinely excelled, however, was in matters of philosophy. He was far ahead of any of the other students and, one suspects, a good few of his examiners.

They also found his knowledge of astronomy impressive, though he harboured some unconventional and potentially dangerous beliefs. He declared that the earth was round and not flat, and that it circulated around the sun once a year. More than a century later, Galileo was destined to be prosecuted for heresy for voicing the same view, but fortunately for

Nostradamus nobody took a fourteen year-old boy seriously enough to persecute him for having eccentric views. His parents, however, were extremely concerned. The family were Christian converts, but they were still Jews by race and as such their position in local society was extremely precarious. The last thing Michel's father needed in his position was to have his headstrong young son airing heretical theories.

By the time he was eighteen, Nostradamus had tired of pure academia. He expressed a wish to become a physician, like his grandfathers before him. There was no faculty of medicine at Avignon and so he enrolled at the University of Montpellier, unquestionably the best school of medicine in France, and possibly the best in Europe. The professors there were among the first to be allowed to dissect corpses to facilitate the effective teaching of anatomy. The Duke of Anjou had extended his permission in 1376 and had allotted them the body of one convicted criminal per annum. This was, of course, totally inadequate for their purposes, but it was better than nothing. Elsewhere in France, anatomical dissection was forbidden as a form of necromancy.

At Montpellier, young Nostradamus was able to attend lectures by the finest physicians in Europe, some of them resident but many visiting from other seats of learning throughout the continent. Medicine had changed little since his grandfathers' day, and still comprised – to modern eyes – a strange mixture of science, alchemy and magic. After three years at the college, Nostradamus was considered ready to graduate.

The examination was oral – written examinations had not been invented – and Nostradamus had to field questions from his professors for four-hour sessions over several days. However, he was an outstanding student and, as before, proved more than equal to their interrogation. They had no hesitation in granting him his degree and he swapped his student's gown for the hooded red robe which survives to this day as a badge of learning in all French academic establishments.

Michel was now a scholar, but not yet a physician. To achieve that, he was obliged to teach for three months under supervision, and then undergo further examinations under four professors. These were followed by a visit to the Chancellor, who took out a massive medical tome, stuck a pin into a page selected at random and questioned the student on the disease covered in that particular passage. Young Nostradamus passed all these tests with consummate ease. He was then presented with an aphorism of Hippocrates and instructed to write a thesis on it by the following morning. He duly presented his paper and was cross-examined on its contents by his professors for four hours. His conclusions were declared sound and, a week later, Nostradamus was presented with his licence to practice medicine by the Bishop of Montpellier.

Nostradamus had only been qualified as a physician for a matter of weeks when disaster hit Montpellier in the form of bubonic plague. We now know that this disease is caused by a bacterium transmitted to humans by fleas who have lived on infected rats. It is a horrifying illness that kills in a few days. The first symptom is a rapid rise in body temperature, followed by vomiting and severe muscular pains; mental disorientation comes next and this quickly degenerates into full-scale delirium. Lymph nodes swell up and become agonisingly painful as they fill with pus. Death is not far away. Even today there are periodic outbreaks of the plague, particularly in Asia, and, if antibiotics are not administered within twelve hours of the first show of symptoms, ninety per cent of victims will die within three days.

Europe was no stranger to epidemics in general and the plague in particular. In the middle of the fourteenth century, as many as one-third of the continent's entire population had been wiped out by the so-called Black Death, and there had been numerous outbreaks in the intervening years, yet the medical profession were no nearer understanding what caused them, let alone how to cure them. Ideas for treatment ranged from the totally useless to the bizarre. Even the doctors' own approach to their patients was odd in the extreme. It was customary for a physician attending a plague victim to clothe himself in a shirt soaked in magical juices and dyed with seven different coloured powders; over this he would wear a leather tunic, supposedly impregnable by the poisoned air surrounding his patient. As further measures of protection, he would wear eye-glasses, tie a sponge over his nose, and clasp some garlic in his mouth.

It is not recorded whether Nostradamus himself adopted this outlandish outfit while attending his patients, but it seems unlikely. It is an odd irony that a man destined to be hailed as one of the world's great prophets should ridicule the mystical mumbo-jumbo which was so much a part of his profession. It is important to remember that Nostradamus was still only in his early twenties and a newly qualified physician, yet he still had the self confidence to set out to develop a new and revolutionary treatment for the plague. He flew in the face of conventional wisdom by refusing to bleed his patients and giving them instead rose pills, a medicine of his own invention. We know precisely what was in them from his own records. They consisted of dried rose petals, ground to a fine powder, and mixed with sawdust, Iris of Florence, cloves, calamus and lignum aloes. He advised his patients to place the `pill' under their tongue and to keep it there without swallowing it. In addition to rose pills, Nostradamus insisted on a rigid regimen of hygiene, clean bedding and unpolluted water.

His new treatment methods elicited reactions ranging from ridicule to outright hostility from his colleagues. Looking at them today, they contained elements, both medicinal and hygienic, which would not only have relieved some of the symptoms of the disease, but also would have gone a long way towards preventing its spread. The people of Montpellier did not know why young Nostradamus's methods worked, and they cared less.

Soon his reputation as a 'plague doctor' spread beyond Montpellier to the surrounding countryside and nearby towns. For the next four years, Nostradamus lived an itinerant existence, travelling from town to town, hamlet to hamlet, wherever the plague struck. As his fame grew, so did his experience and success, and his reputation for unstinting devotion to duty.

Nostradamus stopped his wanderings for a while and settled in the ancient city of Carcasonne, where he ingratiated himself with the powers-that-be by curing the Bishop of various unspecified disorders by means of a pomade of his own design. From Carcasonne he passed to Toulouse, and from there to Narbonne and on to Bordeaux. During his travels, he revisited his old home town of Avignon. Here he settled for a while, and threw himself back into his studies. He worked closely with local apothecaries and widened his clinical experience.

Finally, after four and half years, the epidemic had run its course, and Nostradamus returned to Montpellier to gain his doctorate. When he re-enrolled at the University in October 1529, he was not yet twenty-six years old and a local folk hero. This did nothing to ingratiate him with his professors, who found him arrogant and argumentative. Nostradamus, for his part, believed that much of what he was being taught was wrong, but he learned what was offered to him and managed to toe the establishment line sufficiently for them to award him his doctorate a year later.

Nostradamus set up a practice in Montpellier and immediately attracted a large and lucrative clientele, but he found the whole situation deeply frustrating. Not only was he obliged to teach at the University, he was obliged to teach medical practices which he knew to be either ineffective or damaging. He was also required to administer these same treatments on his own patients, lest he incurred the wrath of the establishment.

One day in the spring of 1531, he decided he had had enough. He packed his books and meagre personal effects on to the back of a mule and set off on his travels again. For the next two years he wandered through Provence and the Languedoc before ending up in Toulouse. It was while he was in that city that he received a letter from Julius Caesar Scalinger, one of the pre-eminent scholars of sixteenth-century Europe. Scalinger, current physician to the Bishop of Agen, wrote that he was interested in some of his ideas and would like to arrange a meeting. Nostradamus was extremely flattered by the invitation and immediately travelled to Agen, where he took up lodgings. The two men hit it off immediately. They were both extremely intelligent, radical thinkers whose interests overlapped and indeed dovetailed.

Scalinger, unlike the wandering Nostradamus, was a happily married man with a beautiful wife and two sons. It is hardly surprising that Nostradamus, now approaching thirty years old, would envy this picture of marital bliss. As a Jew, albeit a Christianised Jew, he had a strong sense of family, a desire to continue the family line. He decided to settle in Agen, establish a practice and find a suitable wife. There was no shortage of candidates. Well-placed fathers in Agen must have seen this celebrated young doctor as a more than suitable son-in-law.

Nostradamus, however, was not a man to have a choice thrust upon him. He fell in love with and married a young woman whose name has never been recorded, but who has been described as 'of high lineage, very beautiful and very agreeable'. She bore him two sons in quick succession and, by all accounts, the couple lived an idyllic family life. It is entirely probable that

Nostradamus would have spent the rest of his days in Agen, practising medicine, conferring with his friend Scalinger, and watching his sons grow. It was not to be, however. In 1537, the plague struck Agen and Nostradamus prepared himself to confront his old adversary on home ground.

His reputation in dealing with the plague was unparalleled, and the entire community looked to him to perform nothing short of a miracle. In the broad sense he succeeded; he certainly saved hundreds, if not thousands in the region. Tragically, his own family were not among them; his wife and two children died of the plague. At a public level, Nostradamus was ridiculed for his arrogance; privately his life was completely shattered. His late wife's family compounded his misery by bringing a law suit against him for the return of her dowry.

The establishment rose up against him in other ways. Everyone suddenly remembered that their erstwhile hero was a Jew. A sculptor came forward with a story which dated back some four years. Apparently, according to his detractor, Nostradamus had been watching a workman casting a bronze sculpture of the Virgin Mary and had remarked that to make such images was to create 'more devils'. It is probable that Nostradamus was merely commenting on the lack of artistic merit in the piece, but in the climate of hate that now surrounded him, he found himself facing accusations of heresy.

The heresy charges against Nostradamus were never, in fact, acted upon, but there was no longer a place for him in Agen. He had no alternative but to return to his role as the wandering Jew. This itinerant phase of his life was destined to last for more than eight years and took him to Guyanne, Lorraine and Italy. His journey was not merely a matter of wanderlust; it was a continuing quest for knowledge. Everywhere he went, he consulted with eminent physicians and apothecaries. The majority of these, though practising Christianity, were, like himself of Jewish extraction. It was during this period that Nostradamus's gift for prophecy first manifested itself, or at least this was the time that others first became aware of it.

Initially the gift took the form of second sight, a form of telepathy common among Highland Scots, a phenomenon they refer to as being 'fey'. There are several anecdotes about Nostradamus which illustrate this gift. On one occasion, during his time in Italy, Nostradamus was walking along a road in Ancona when he encountered a group of young Franciscan monks. He stood aside to allow them to pass and then suddenly prostrated himself at the feet of one of the young men. When the startled monk, whose name was Felix Peretti, asked Nostradamus what he was doing, the prophet replied that he was kneeling before His Holiness. This caused much embarrassment to Peretti, a former swineherd from a local village, and considerable amusement to his colleagues. As they went on their way, leaving Nostradamus on his knees, they assumed he was either drunk or insane. He was neither. Father Peretti was destined to become the Cardinal of Montalato, and in 1585, twenty years after Nostradamus's death, he was elected Pope Sixtus IV.

On another celebrated occasion, Nostradamus

was staying with one Seigneur de Florinville at his castle in Lorraine. Florinville had heard tales of his guest's extraordinary psychic abilities, but was extremely sceptical about them, and decided to put them to the test. The two men were walking through the farmyard of the castle when Florinville pointed out two pigs in a pen, one white, one black, and asked what would become of them. Nostradamus answered without hesitation that the white pig would be eaten by a wolf, and the black pig would be eaten by Florinville himself.

Florinville set about making sure the prediction did not come true. He sent word to the castle kitchen that the white pig should be slaughtered immediately and served for supper that evening. The cook duly killed it, dressed it, and put it on a spit, ready for roasting. By chance, two children who lived on the estate had caught a young wolf and were endeavouring to tame it. The animal got loose, made its way to the castle kitchen and started to devour the pig. By the time the cook returned to the kitchen, the young wolf had made substantial inroads into the carcass. The cook hastily buried the remains, slaughtered the black pig and cooked it in its place.

At dinner that night, Florinville gloatingly told Nostradamus that his prediction had been wrong and that they were at this very minute eating the white pig. Unabashed, Nostradamus insisted that they were in fact eating the black pig. Florinville summoned the cook and ordered him to bring the white pig to the table to prove his point. The embarrassed cook was forced to confess all. From that time on Seigneur de Florinville was a sceptic no longer.

When Nostradamus was staying with a family called Beauveau near Orléans, he was working in his study when there was a loud banging on the door. Irritated by the interruption, he went over, opened the door and found himself faced with a very distressed family servant. Before the young man could say anything, Nostradamus told him, 'You are making a lot of fuss over a lost dog. Go to the road to Orléans. You will find the dog there on its leash.' The young servant backed away, astonished. He had indeed lost a dog; not any dog, but his master's prize wolfhound. He ran down to the Orléans road and sure enough, there he found the animal being led back to the house on its leash.

These stories, and legions more like them, spread around France, increasing Nostradamus's already considerable celebrity. Many of them were no doubt apocryphal, and even if they were true, they were no more than parlour tricks compared with the written prophecies he was to produce in later life.

In 1544, Nostradamus, now 40 years old, was summoned to Marseilles, where there was yet another outbreak of the plague. Working alongside another celebrated physician, Louis Serres, he achieved his now customary level of success. Over the years he had refined his methods of treatment by a mixture of acute observation and trial and error. His methods, once ridiculed, were now employed by most far-sighted physicians in Europe. The plague abated in a matter of months and Nostradamus decided to settle in Marseilles. It was a city which had a lot to offer him. Being a seaport, it gave him access to all manner of herbs and medications unavailable in inland cities, while there were excellent libraries and apothecaries. However, two years later he was on the move again, fighting the plague, firstly in Aix-en-Provence, then in Salon and Lyons. Wherever Nostradamus went, his work was outstandingly successful and grateful citizens showered him with honours, money and gifts.

In Lyons, Nostradamus once again thought he had found a place to settle, but he was virtually hounded out of town by a rival physician, Antoine Sarrazin. Sarrazin, jealous of Nostradamus's celebrity and aware of his Semitic origins, started to spread rumours about his rival, claiming that he practised magic. The people of Lyons were so grateful to Nostradamus for delivering them from the plague that they were unwilling to act against him, but the situation became so intolerable that he eventually left of his own volition.

In 1547, he returned to Salon, the scene of his own personal tragedy. Ten years seem to have healed some of the wounds and he decided that he was ready to embark on a second marriage. Four months after arriving in the city, on 11 November 1547, he married a young widow called Anne Ponsart Gemelle. The couple set up home in a large house in an alley off Place de la Ponsierre, and it was here that Nostradamus was to spend the rest of his days. His wandering was over at last.

The house itself was tall, with a spiral staircase leading up to an attic, a room which Nostradamus elected to use as his study. It was here that the *Centuries* and his other prophecies would be written, but not yet. During his first few years in Salon, Nostradamus continued to practice as a physician, but the town was small and patients few. This did not bother Nostradamus.

He had adequate means, his new wife was a woman of substance, and the situation afforded ample time to pursue his research and writing.

In 1550, Nostradamus published his first book. It was an almanac predicting events for the coming year. The subjects covered in the book were fairly mundane – the weather, harvests, and so on – certainly nothing to incur the wrath of the Church Inquisitors. The almanac proved extremely popular, and Nostradamus continued to publish one a year until his death. To students of his more serious prophecies, the most interesting feature of these early almanacs is their literary form. Each book contained twelve four line poems, or quatrains, a style which he would continue to employ in all his major works.

Nostradamus' first full-length work was not remotely prophetic. It was a book on herbal remedies and beauty products. Published in 1552 under the title *Traite des Fardemens* [A Treatise on Make-Up], it was concerned primarily with unguents, cosmetics, love potions and jam, a bizarre change of direction for a man who had spent a quarter of a century battling with the horrors of the plague. One suspects, however, that there were deeper things going through the great man's mind as he sat in his study at night, things that he was not yet ready to put before the world.

It is entirely possible that the prophecies of Nostradamus might never have seen the light of day had it not been for the intervention of one man. Jean-Aymes de Chavigny arrived, unannounced, at Nostradamus's home in Salon in the autumn of 1553. He told the prophet that he had recently abandoned his career as a lawyer and intended to study judicial astrology and prophecy. He had consulted with his old Greek professor, Jean Dorat, a friend and admirer of Nostradamus, and had been advised by him to travel to Salon and apprentice himself to the master. There is no record of how Nostradamus initially reacted to this suggestion, but what is certain is that, within a matter of months, Chavigny had become his disciple, secretary and editor. He would later become his biographer, and it is from Chavigny's writings that much of what we know about the life of Nostradamus derives.

NOSTRADAMUS THE PROPHET

Jean-Aymes de Chavigny must have gained his new master's trust in very short order, because it was in him that Nostradamus first confided his concept for the *Centuries*. His plan was to write a book prophesying the future of mankind. It was to be constructed in ten individual volumes, each containing one hundred individual predictions – hence the name of the work. The prophecies would be presented in the form of quatrains, the four-lined poems he had already used in his almanacs. He showed Chavigny a great body of work which he had completed over the previous five years. It told of wars, famines, the rise and fall of the great houses of Europe, murder, and deceit. The *Centuries* were a blueprint for the future of Europe and beyond.

In his biography of Nostradamus, Chavigny explains his master's initial reluctance to publish the *Centuries*: 'He kept them a long time without wishing to print them, thinking that the novelty of the matter would not fail to arouse infinite detractions, calumnies and attacks more than venomous, as indeed it transpired. In the end, vanquished by the desire which he had to be useful to the public, he published them; and immediately their noise and renown rang through the mouths of our compatriots and of strangers with great wonder.'

Motivated by the wish to do good, and encouraged by Chavigny, Nostradamus agreed to allow the first edition of the *Centuries* to be published in April 1555. Marce Bonhomme, a printer from Lyons, was entrusted with the production. This first edition was a slim volume which contained only the first three complete cycles of 100 quatrains, together with 53 quatrains of the fourth.

The books were an instant success, which is surprising for a number of reasons. To many readers they must have been totally unintelligible, written as they were in a mixture of French, Greek and Latin. And even those who had the scholarship to translate them were faced with verses which were at best obscure, and often impenetrable. In addition, Nostradamus employed anagrams, abbreviations, puns and all manner of literary devices to confuse his readers further. He apparently possessed no sense of syntax or grammar, and on the surface the quatrains were a complete mess. One might find this surprising when one considers that the author was a man of vast education, but the reason is simple. He intended them to be obscure, as he explained in a preface, written in the form of a letter to his infant son, César.

'Although for a long time I have predicted a long time in advance what has afterwards come to pass, I was willing to be silent and pass over what might be harmful, not only as relates to the present day, but for the greater part of future time ... If I were to relate what will happen in the future, governors, secretaries and ecclesiastics would find it in so little accord with their fancies that they would immediately condemn what future centuries I know and perceive to be true ... This has been the cause which has led me to withhold my tongue from the vulgar, and my pen from paper. Then I thought I would enlarge a little, touching the Vulgar Advent, and show by abstruse and twisted sentences the future causes, even the most urgent, as I perceived them, whatever changes might be, so only as not to scandalise them, and write down everything in a cloudy fashion, rather than plainly prophetic.' It is clear from this passage that Nostradamus' main motive for obscurity was to save his own hide. He felt that if his prophecies were too baldly stated, and they turned out to be true, he might well be accused of heresy.

The Vulgar Advent he mentions in his preface is the French Revolution, more than 200 years in the future. Some of his most straightforward and accurate quatrains deal with this catastrophic period in French history, and do so in great detail, naming names, describing locations, even providing exact dates. Since he knew he would be long dead before the `Vulgar Advent', and had nothing to fear from its perpetrators, it is hardly surprising that he did not feel the need to be obscure about his predictions on this subject as he did in matters of his own time.

In a further attempt to distance himself from accusations of sorcery, Nostradamus included a not very subtle passage to his son begging him not to become involved with the occult, thereby distancing himself from it by association. 'And further, my son, I implore you not to attempt to employ your understanding in such reveries and vanities which wither the body and bring the soul into perdition, troubling the feeble sense: even the vanity of that most execrable magic, denounced already by the Sacred Scriptures and by the Divine Canons of the Church.'

Despite his protestations to the contrary, there is absolutely no doubt that Nostradamus called on astrology and other practices frowned on by the Church while compiling his prophecies. His quatrains are littered with astrological and astronomical references; in fact, they were his preferred method of providing dates for his predictions. And as for magic, it was part of his Jewish heritage. Consider, for instance, the first two quatrains of the first Century, where he describes his own working practices.

Seated alone in the secret study,
At night on a brazen tripod.
A slender flame lights my solitude
And makes possible that which would have been in vain.

(CENTURY 1 – QUATRAIN 1)

The wand in his hand is placed upon the tripod.
He moistens the hem of his garment and his foot.
He hears voices and trembles with fear.
In divine splendour, a god sits beside him.

(CENTURY 1 – QUATRAIN 2)

At first glance, both these quatrains can be interpreted in a totally innocent fashion – innocent, that is, in the eyes of the Church in sixteenth-century France. It is quite reasonable to picture a great thinker sitting alone at night in his secret study. The 'brazen tripod' could be nothing more sinister than a three-legged stool, and the 'slender flame' would certainly make the impossible possible – it would enable Nostradamus to see in the dark. The second quatrain is not quite so easy to explain away, but many tried it. The 'wand' has often been interpreted as a pen dripping with ink, and the last two lines of the quatrain as merely implying that, in a state of deep meditation, the prophet was visited by the inspiration of the Almighty.

As James Laver explains in his book *Nostradamus the Prophet*, this simply does not stand up to close scrutiny. He quotes a passage from *De Mysteries Egyptiorum* [Concerning Egyptian Mysteries], a book on Chaldean and Assyrian magic written in the fourth century by Jamblinchus. It describes an ancient ritual which mirrors exactly what Nostradamus describes in his second quatrain. 'The prophetess of Branchus sits in the sanctuary, holds in her hand a wand, bathes her foot and the hem of her robe in water and by these means she is filled with the divine illumination and, finding herself in communication with the divinity, she prophesies.'

It is simply inconceivable that this is a coincidence. Nostradamus was clearly on intimate terms with the fourth-century manuscript. It is probable that he was also familiar with *De Daemonibus* [Concerning Demons], a twelfth-century magical tract by Michael Psellus, which states that 'The diviners take a basin of water suitable for the use of deamons. The water seems first to vibrate as if it were about to emit sounds. The water does not differ in appearance from normal water, but it has a property of being able to compose verse, which renders it eminently apt to receive the prophetic spirit ... later, when the water appears to boil and spill over, a faint voice murmurs words which will contain the revelation of future events.'

Whether or not Nostradamus actually owned either of these books will never be known. They were not exactly on the Church Inquisitors' required reading list, and he would hardly admit to having them. So, was the prophet really a black magician? It is highly improbable. What is more likely is that he used or adapted these ancient rituals as a means of inducing a trance. Staring into a bowl of water or at a candle is little different from the techniques employed by present-day hypnotists, and Nostradamus freely admits in his writings that most of his prophecies came to him in a trance-like state.

THE CENTURIES

Within a matter of months after the publication of the first volume of the *Centuries*, Nostradamus was a household name among the nobility and educated classes of French society. His fame reached Paris, and more particularly the court of King Henri II and his wife Catherine de' Medici. The queen in particular, although outwardly a devout Catholic, was fascinated with the occult, and even retained a court astrologer, Luc Gauric.

Some months before she read Nostradamus's prophecies, Gauric had warned the Queen that her husband should avoid competing in a tournament in his 41st year. It was with some discomfort, therefore, that Catherine read a quatrain in *Centuries* which seemed to confirm Gauric's warning in graphic detail.

> **The young lion shall overcome the older**
> **On the field of combat by single combat.**
> **In a golden cage he shall put out his eye,**
> **Two wounds from one, then he shall die a cruel death.**

(CENTURY 1 – QUATRAIN 35)

Catherine showed the quatrain to her husband and, even though he did not share her enthusiasm for the occult, he was obviously disturbed by the apparent similarities between the two predictions of Nostradamus and Gauric. Nostradamus was duly summoned to Paris from Salon. Nostradamus reached the capital in less than four weeks – half the normal journey time – because, in her anxiety to discuss the matter with the prophet, Catherine arranged for fresh horses to be waiting at every staging post. He arrived at court late on the night of 15 August 1556, and, early the following morning, was escorted to the royal country residence at St-Germain-en-Laye.

He was greeted by the king and queen in their private chambers and Catherine asked him to explain the quatrain in question. There is no record of Nostradamus's reply, but it is likely that it was vague and tactful. Whatever he said, it failed to impress the King, who left the meeting after a few minutes. Catherine, on the other hand, wanted to talk at length. Nostradamus and Catherine spent several hours together, discussing astrology, prophecy and destiny. It is unlikely that either of them would have chosen to stray onto the ultra-controversial subject of magic at this stage, but there is no question that they did so at a later date.

Catherine insisted that Nostradamus remain in Paris so that they could consult on such matters at greater length. She arranged for him to stay at the palace of the Archbishop of Sens in Paris. His reward for his travels and efforts in pecuniary terms was modest. The King sent him a purse of 100 crowns, which barely covered his travelling costs. The prophet soon recovered from this temporary financial setback, however. Word of his royal patronage spread around Paris like wildfire, and members of the court and those merely aspiring to social position were soon banging at his door, offering outrageous sums of money for advice, predictions and horoscopes.

Nostradamus found that his new celebrity status in the capital had its dangers. Word reached him that the Justices of Paris were planning to interrogate him about his use of magic. The prophet had no doubt that it was in fact the Inquisition which wanted to get its hands on him, and he immediately packed his bags and fled back to the relative safety of Salon.

On his return home, he found himself thrust into the role of a local hero, and his house was inundated with would-be clients and well-wishers. All this was very gratifying, but it did distract him from his primary task, which was to complete the last three cycles of *Centuries*. This he finally succeeded in doing in the autumn of 1558. A few copies were printed but, for the sake of self-preservation, Nostradamus prevented them from being widely circulated in his lifetime.

The reputation of Nostradamus as the world's greatest prophet was consolidated the following year when King Henri II was killed in a tragic accident at a tournament. As Nostradamus had predicted, he was pierced through the eye with a lance and died an agonising and protracted death as the result of his injuries. Opinion was sharply divided about the prophet. At one end of the scale, in Paris, an angry mob gathered in the streets, burned an effigy of him, and demanded that the Church Inquisitors try him as a heretic.

At court, however, the reaction was quite the opposite. Queen Catherine in no way held Nostradamus responsible for her husband's death. To her the accident, tragic though it was, merely served to confirm what she had said all along, that Nostradamus was a great prophet. Her courtiers, previously extremely sceptical, now became avid readers of the quatrains. One in particular caught their eye. It appeared to refer to the new boy king, Francis II, and his marriage to Mary Stuart of Scotland.

The first born of the widow of an unfortunate marriage
Will have no children and two islands will be
thrown into turmoil.
Before the age of eighteen, while still a minor,
Of the other, even younger, will be a betrothal.

(CENTURY 10 - QUATRAIN 39)

Once again, the prophecy was fulfilled. Francis, who had always been a sickly child, died shortly before his eighteenth birthday, without producing an heir. Then, one by one, the other lines of the quatrains became reality. Mary Stuart, Francis's widow, returned to her native country, and became Mary Queen of Scots, thus throwing France and England into a 'turmoil'. Then, a year later, Charles IX, Francis's younger brother, became engaged to Elizabeth of Austria at the age of eleven.

While Catherine de' Medici remained a loyal supporter of Nostradamus, others started to view him with deep suspicion. Books and papers began to appear that denounced the prophet as a heretic. Even in Salon, he received death threats; his house was stoned by a mob of young Catholic extremists. He became so afraid for the safety of his family that, for a short period, he demanded voluntary imprisonment.

In time, the furore abated, but Nostradamus continued to live a reclusive existence. Aided by the ever faithful Chavigny, he wrote copiously, but published nothing. Then, in 1564, he was forced into the limelight once again. Catherine de' Medici, now Regent of France, was making a tour of her kingdom, accompanied by her teenage son, Charles IX. Catherine insisted that the royal party make a special visit to Salon, with the specific purpose of meeting with Nostradamus. The audience was duly arranged at the papal mansion, where Nostradamus spent several hours with Catherine and the young king, drawing up horoscopes for various members of the Valois family.

Before leaving Salon, Charles bestowed on Nostradamus the title of Counsellor and Physician in Ordinary to the court, together with the relevant salary and privileges. This official mark of royal acclaim should have freed him to publish again without

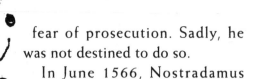

fear of prosecution. Sadly, he was not destined to do so.

In June 1566, Nostradamus suffered a severe attack of gout, painful but not in itself life threatening. The prophet knew better. He sensed his end was near and set about putting his affairs in order. He spent his last days in his study, where Chavigny had erected a special bench to allow his master to move his crippled body around. This bench was the subject of a prediction he had made to Chavigny more than a decade earlier. In 1554, Nostradamus had described a dream to his assistant in which he had seen that 'close friends and family would find him completely dead near a bed and a bench.'

On the night of 1 July 1566, Chavigny wished his master good night, but Nostradamus assured him that he would be dead before sunrise. When Chavigny returned to his room the following morning, together with his wife, son and two friends, he found Nostradamus's body lying on the floor between the bed and the bench.

Even in death, Nostradamus continued to amaze. All his life he had had a phobia about people walking on his grave, and he left instructions that he should be buried, upright, in the wall of the local church of Cordeliers. His widow, Anne, saw to it that his wishes were followed to the letter, and there, one would have thought, the story would have ended. But Nostradamus's fame continued to grow after his death, and rumours began to circulate that there were unpublished manuscripts buried in his coffin. These, of course, would have been of immense value. In 1700, bowing to pressure from academics, the municipal authorities of Salon gave permission for the body to be exhumed. The coffin was opened. There were no manuscripts inside, but the skeletal remains of the prophet were adorned with a gold medallion which he had donned on the night of his death. Inscribed on the medallion was the date, 1700.

CHAPTER 1

PREDICTIONS FOR HIS OWN TIME

M ost of Nostradamus's predictions pertaining to the sixteenth century centred around French domestic issues, and more specifically on the French royal family, the House of Valois, headed by King Henri II and his queen, Catherine de' Medici.

KING HENRI II

**The great Chyren [Henri II] will be chief of the world,
Beyond all others, loved, feared and dreaded.
His fame and praise go beyond the heavens,
And will be greatly satisfied with the title of victor.**

(CENTURY 6 – QUATRAIN 70)

This particular quatrain is generally considered to refer to King Henri II of France. Henri and his wife, Catherine de' Medici, were Nostradamus's great champions and, while they were not patrons in the strictest sense of the word, they lent him considerable credibility at court and beyond. They also protected him from the attentions of the Inquisition.

It is a matter of historical fact that King Henri had a weakness for flattery, and here Nostradamus slakes that particular thirst. It would be wrong to consider this quatrain as a prophecy. It is more an act of political opportunism by Nostradamus, particularly in light of the fact that he already published a quatrain which predicted that Henri would meet an untimely death at a tournament, and was not therefore destined to fulfil his true potential.

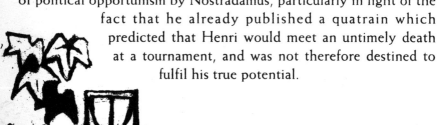

THE DEATH OF HENRI II

The young lion shall overcome the older
On the field of combat by single combat.
In a golden cage he shall put out his eye.
Two wounds from one, then he shall die a cruel death.

(CENTURY 1 – QUATRAIN 35)

This quatrain, predicting the death of Henri II, was published in 1556, three years prior to the monarch's death, and is perhaps the most celebrated of all Nostradamus's prophecies. It is one of the few upon which his many interpreters, both contemporary and modern, are in total agreement.

On 30 June 1559, Henri was celebrating a double marriage; that of his daughter, Elizabeth, to Philip II of Spain, and that of his sister, Marguerite, to the Duke of Savoy. To mark the occasion, a tournament was held on the rue St Antoine outside Paris. Henri had been specifically warned against jousting in his 41st year, but chose to ignore the advice.

Henri's opponent was Gabrie' Count of Montgomery, captain of his Scottish Guard. In their first joust, Henri was nearly unseated. He wanted a second tilt, but his opponent, aware of Nostradamus's prophecy, tried to decline. The king, however, insisted. The crowd fell silent as the two combatants wheeled their horses and charged down the lists towards one another. There was a loud crack as Montgomery's lance shattered against Henri's shield. A splinter of wood pierced the king's golden visor and lodged behind his left eye, blinding him and penetrating his brain. After ten days of agony, he died.

On the night of the king's death, a mob gathered in the streets of Paris and demanded that the Church Inquisitors arrest Nostradamus as a heretic. In court circles, however, this one prophecy convinced many sceptics of the prophet's powers.

THE WIDOW CATHERINE

**The lady shall be left alone in the kingdom
By the death of her husband on the field of honour.
Seven years she will express her grief and weeping,
Then a long life with good fortune for her realm.**

(CENTURY 6 – QUATRAIN 63)

After Henri II's untimely death, his widow, Catherine, continued to champion Nostradamus, and increasingly relied upon his prophecies for personal guidance. She was particularly anxious to know the fate of her seven surviving children and the prophet wrote several quatrains on them and on the fate of the Valois dynasty.

Written immediately after the king's death in 1559, this quatrain is another example of Nostradamus's political opportunism. He painted a glowing future for his champion. Catherine, knowing the prophecy, played her part in making it come true.

While it is unlikely that Catherine was deeply in love with her late husband, who spent more time with his mistress than he did with her, Catherine did indeed mourn him until August 1566, seven years after his death. She lived on as Regent and survived to an old age by sixteenth-century standards. She died on 5 January 1589, shortly before her 70th birthday.

When the serpents encircle the altar,
And the Trojan blood is troubled by the Spanish,
Because of them a great number shall perish.
The leader will flee, and hide in the marshes.

(CENTURY 1 – QUATRAIN 19)

When Henri II died, Catherine de' Medici changed her coat of arms. The new emblem was a snake, curled round a star, and biting its own tail. 'Trojan blood' is a metaphor used by Nostradamus on several occasions in his quatrains. It refers to royal blood, based on a commonly held myth that the French royal family were directly descended from King Priam of Troy. The French conflict with Spain did not in fact happen for another thirty years, until the interregnum of 1589, and the subsequent war of the Spanish succession.

CATHERINE'S CHILDREN

The holy widow hears the news
Of her offspring in trouble and distress.
He who quarrels by his pursuit,
Will make the shaven heads pile up.

(CENTURY 6 – QUATRAIN 29)

In this quatrain Nostradamus warns Catherine that her children
will have turbulent lives. The massacre of St Bartholomew and the
murder of the brothers Guise by her son, Henri III, would, he
predicted, combine to spark off a civil war between the Leaguers,
a Catholic association, and the Protestant Huguenots.

The first born of the widow of an unfortunate marriage
Will have no children and two islands will be
thrown into turmoil.
Before the age of eighteen, while still a minor,
Of the other, even younger, will be a betrothal.

(CENTURY 10 – QUATRAIN 39)

This verse refers to the marriage of Catherine
de' Medici's eldest son, Francis II, to Mary
Stuart, later Mary Queen of Scots, in 1558.
Francis was only sixteen at the time of the

marriage, which was, as Nostradamus predicted, unhappy and childless. When Francis died in 1560, still only seventeen, Mary returned to Scotland. This caused discord between France and England.

The third line of the quatrain refers to Francis's younger brother, later Charles IX, who was betrothed to Elizabeth of Austria when he was only eleven years old.

> **The unhappy marriage will be celebrated**
> **With great joy, but it will end in unhappiness.**
> **Mary and her mother-in-law will detest one another.**
> **With Phybe [Francis II] dead, the in-law shall**
> **be more piteous.**

(Century 10 – Quatrain 55)

This quatrain also refers to the marriage between Francis II and Mary Queen of Scots. It is well documented that Catherine de' Medici loathed her daughter-in-law, and that the feeling was mutual. Mary took great pleasure in describing Catherine as 'the merchant's daughter'.

A coffin shall be placed in an iron cage,
Where the King's seven children are held.
The spirit of their ancestors will rise from their graves,
Sorrowing to see the fruit of their line dead.

(CENTURY 1 – QUATRAIN 10)

Catherine de' Medici had seven surviving children at the time of her husband's death in 1559. Nostradamus accurately predicted that they would be the last of the Valois line, when he had a vision of the final coffin placed behind the iron grille in the vault at St Denis which already held the remains of the rest of the ill-fated family. Their ancestors, he felt, would rise up like ghosts to mourn the end of their dynasty.

From seven branches, they shall be reduced to three
The older ones will be surprised by death.
Two of them will be attracted to fratricide,
But the conspirators will die in their beds.

(CENTURY 6 – QUATRAIN 11)

The seven branches in this quatrain were, of course, Catherine's seven children. By 1575, only François, Henri and Marguerite were still alive. François and Henri were 'attracted to fratricide' in the sense that they were behind the assassination of the brothers de Guise.

There is also a suggestion that their

rivalry was so intense that they plotted to kill one another. Henri certainly accused his brother of plotting against him and warned him that such treachery warranted a sentence of death. This was no empty threat. He enlisted the help of his brother-in-law, Henri de Navarre, to rid the court of François. Despite all their plotting, however, both brothers contrived to die in their sleep.

Marguerite married Henri de Navarre, but, despite having a reputation for sexual insatiability, never managed to conceive. She died childless at the age of fifty-three, and with her died the Valois line.

MONTGOMERY'S FATE

He who in a struggle with a weapon in a deed of war
Had carried off the prize from his better;
By night, six shall abuse him in his bed.
Naked and without armour, he shall be suddenly surprised.

(CENTURY 3 – QUATRAIN 30)

This quatrain predicts the fate of the unfortunate Count of Montgomery, who accidentally killed his friend Henri II. Although the king had forgiven him on his death bed, Catherine de' Medici was not inclined to be so reasonable. She demanded his life, and so Montgomery fled to England as a Huguenot. He returned to Normandy a decade later to lead the

Protestant rebellion. After a measure of success, Montgomery and his army were defeated by Marshal de Mantignon at Domfort. His life was spared as a condition of his surrender, but Catherine de' Medici still held a grudge against him. She ordered six men of the Royal Guard to arrest him, and he was kidnapped from his bed on the night of 27 May 1574.

THE REIGN OF HENRI III

In the years that the one eyed king shall reign in France,
The court shall have great trouble.
The great man from Blois will kill his friend,
The kingdom shall be in an evil way, and double doubt.

(CENTURY 3 – QUATRAIN 55)

The one eyed king in this quatrain is Henri II of France, mortally wounded in a joust in 1559 when a wood splinter pierced his eye. The second two lines refer to his heir, Henri III, who arranged for the assassination of the de Guise brothers at Blois. Their murder caused considerable civil unrest, and the 'double doubt' refers to the two factions involved – the Leaguers and the King's supporters.

A DOUBLE ASSASSINATION

**In Paris, a plot is hatched to commit a terrible murder.
It is in Blois that it will happen.
The people of Orléans will want to restore their leader,
Angers, Troyes and Langres will make them pay dearly.**

(CENTURY 3 – QUATRAIN 51)

This quatrain describes the conflict between the Leaguers and the protestant Huguenots. The League was a Catholic association formed in 1568 by Henri, Duke of Guise. Henri III proclaimed himself head of the League, but the duke held on to his own long-established leadership tenaciously, using the association as a platform for his schemes to usurp the throne of France.

Henri felt he had no option but to rid himself of his rival and he ordered his assassination. The duke and his brother, Louis, Cardinal of Lorraine, were murdered at Blois by a member of the king's bodyguard on 23 December 1588.

Immediately after the murder of the brothers, the people of Orléans rose up against the governor, Balzac d'Entragues, and he was replaced by a prominent Leaguer and de Guise supporter, Charles de Lorraine.

They will repent too late,
That he did not put his rival to death.
But he will soon realise
That greater things will cause his line to die.

(CENTURY 1 – QUATRAIN 36)

This quatrain refers to Henri III and his determination to rid French politics of the influence of the de Guise family. Henri ordered the assassination of the duke and his brother, Louis, in 1588, but he allowed another brother, the Duke of Mayenne, to survive. Henri would live to regret his clemency, because, in reality, it was Mayenne who was the ringleader of the de Guise plot to usurp the French throne.

THE PARISIAN PLOT

The people of Paris and their government
Will not tolerate severe repression.
The king will be summoned by trumpets to leave the city.
A ladder shall be put to the wall, and the city will repent.

(CENTURY 3 – QUATRAIN 50)

In 1588, the Leaguers took control of Paris in the name of the people, and drove Henri III and his followers from the city. The king responded to this expulsion by joining forces with his brother-in-law, the Huguenot Henri de Navarre – later to be

Henri IV of France – and planning a siege on Paris. However, Henri III was assassinated before the plan could be put into action.

THE ASSASSINATION OF HENRI III

That which neither weapon nor fire could achieve,
Shall be done with a smooth tongue in council.
In sleep, a dream will make the king think,
He will see the enemy not in war or military blood.

(CENTURY 4 – QUATRAIN 60)

By the end of 1588, Henri III was universally despised and there were calls for his death from all quarters. But, as Nostradamus predicts in this quatrain, the king was not to die in battle but in council. His killer was a Dominican friar, Brother Clément, who managed to obtain a private audience with Henri in his bed chamber on the pretext of delivering a secret message. He leaned over the king's bed and stabbed him in the stomach. Henri died the following day, having named Henri de Navarre as his heir.

It was not only Nostradamus that had predicted this event. Three days before his death, the king foresaw his own demise in a dream. He had a vision of his royal regalia – crown, sceptre and sword – being trodden under foot by a mob led by a monk.

HENRI IV AND THE HOUSE OF NAVARRE

The completion of a great action thwarted,
The name of the seventh shall be that of the fifth.
The third person, a greater foreign warmonger.
Paris will not preserve Paris or Aix.

(CENTURY 2 – QUATRAIN 88)

This is a complex quatrain. Henri III was Catherine de' Medici's fifth child and became the seventh and last king of the Valois line. His sister, Marguerite, married Henri of Navarre, later Henri IV, who was considered a foreigner because Navarre was a principality apart from France. As Nostradamus predicted, Henri IV did indeed become a great warmonger. He besieged Paris to establish his rule in 1590.

THE BATTLE OF IVRY

The French will subdue Ausonne,
While the Pau, Marne and Seine will intoxicate.
He who raises a wall against them,
And the great one will lose his life
from the least to the wall.

(CENTURY 2 – QUATRAIN 63)

This quatrain refers to the battle of Ivry. In 1590, the Duke of Parma was recalled to France from the Netherlands by the Leaguers to fight against Henri de Navarre, who had made a claim on the French throne. The two armies met at Ivry in 1590 and the Duke of Parma was soundly defeated. As Nostradamus predicted, the duke did indeed eventually die in combat.

THE SIEGE OF PARIS

**From Bourges-la-Reine, they will not come
straight to Chartres.
They will rest near Pont d'Anthony,
Then, thanks to seven conspirators,
They will enter Paris which had been closed.**

(CENTURY 9 – QUATRAIN 86)

In this quatrain, Nostradamus predicts the siege of Paris by Henri IV. On 1 November 1589, Henri attacked the left bank, but his advance was halted at the gate of St. Germain. He abandoned the siege and marched south. His subsequent capture of Etampes and occupation of the Beauce region allowed him to surround the city completely and cut off the inhabitants' food supply.

In 1593, Henri looked out over Paris from Montmartre. It was not long before the citizens of the city, anxious to regain their creature comforts, were ready to surrender to him, but the authorities still denied him access to the city.

His claim to the throne was gaining credibility, particularly as he had converted to Catholicism, and the people of Orléans and Bourges threw in their lot with him; Picardy was on the verge of joining them. To hasten the process, Henri had himself crowned with due pomp and ceremony at Chartres. Thenceforth, Henri of Navarre was Henri IV, King of France. On 22 March 1594, he entered Paris. The seven conspirators mentioned in the quatrain were Parisian aristocrats and officials who rallied to his cause.

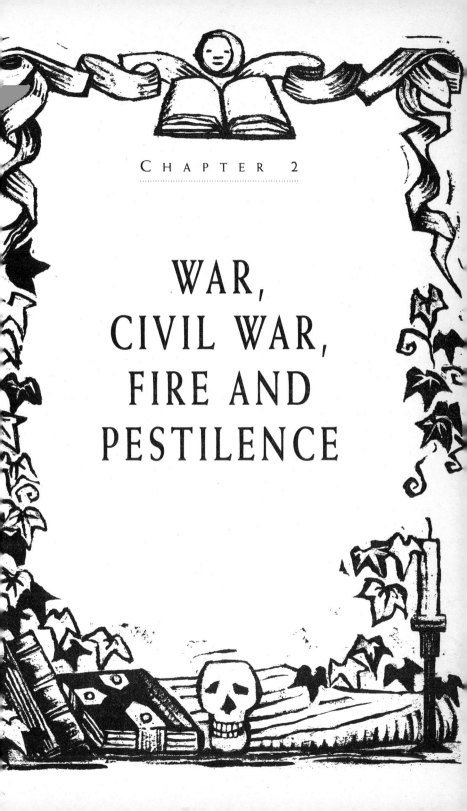

CHAPTER 2

WAR, CIVIL WAR, FIRE AND PESTILENCE

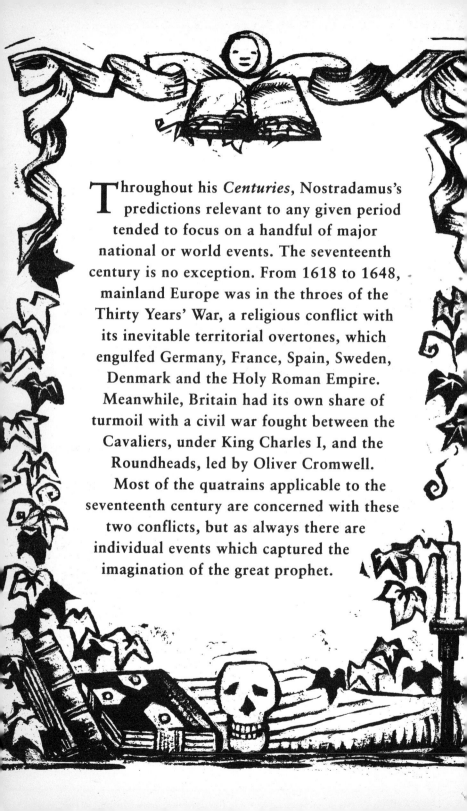

Throughout his *Centuries*, Nostradamus's predictions relevant to any given period tended to focus on a handful of major national or world events. The seventeenth century is no exception. From 1618 to 1648, mainland Europe was in the throes of the Thirty Years' War, a religious conflict with its inevitable territorial overtones, which engulfed Germany, France, Spain, Sweden, Denmark and the Holy Roman Empire. Meanwhile, Britain had its own share of turmoil with a civil war fought between the Cavaliers, under King Charles I, and the Roundheads, led by Oliver Cromwell.

Most of the quatrains applicable to the seventeenth century are concerned with these two conflicts, but as always there are individual events which captured the imagination of the great prophet.

EUROPE AND THE THIRTY YEARS' WAR

THE BATTLE OF AUGSBURG

By Lake Geneva there shall be a plot,
Led by a foreign woman to betray the city.
Before she is killed, her retinue will come to Augsburg,
From where they will invade the people of the Rhine.

(CENTURY 5 – QUATRAIN 12)

This quatrain is generally thought to refer to the defeat of
Bernhard, Duke of Saxe-Weimar, during the Thirty Years' War.
The duke's army was forced to retreat across the
Rhine, leaving southern and central Germany at the
mercy of the army of Ferdinand II, the Holy
Roman Emperor. After Augsburg, all
the major cities along the Rhine fell to
Emperor Ferdinand.

THE SIEGE OF NIMES

Near the aqueduct of Uzes by Gard,
Through the forest and inaccessible mountains,
In the centre of the bridge, he shall be tied by the wrist;
The leader of Nîmes will be very terrible.

(CENTURY 5 – QUATRAIN 58)

In 1627, the Duke of Rohan went to the support of his fellow Protestants who were under siege at the French city of Nîmes. He moved his artillery into the city by taking them across the famous Roman viaduct, the Pont du Gard, which runs from Uzes to Nîmes. When Rohan finally entered the city, he assumed command of the combined Protestant armies.

THE TREATY OF WESTPHALIA

In fury, the Roman king will want to attack Belgium,
Using an army of barbarian soldiers.
In gnashing rage, he will pursue the savages
From Hungary right down to Gibraltar.

(CENTURY 5 – QUATRAIN 13)

The Roman king in this quatrain is Ferdinand II, the Holy Roman Emperor, who joined forces with King Philip of Spain against the combined Protestant powers of Sweden, Denmark and Norway.

In 1648, the Treaty of Westphalia was promulgated. This recognised, among other provisions, the sovereignty of the United Netherlands, the approximate equivalent of modern day Belgium. The 'barbarian soldiers' used to enforce this treaty were German Protestants. France and Spain refused to recognise the treaty, however, and fighting continued for another eleven years, spreading as far south as Gibraltar, before finally being brought to an end, in 1659, by the Peace of the Pyrenees.

THE FRONDE WARS

French fleet, you must not approach Corsica,
Much less Sardinia, or you will regret it. You will all die,
Deprived of help because of the Fronde.
The sea will become bloodstained, but the prisoner will
doubt me.

(CENTURY 3 – QUATRAIN 87)

This is an unusual quatrain. Rather than presenting a piece of reportage, Nostradamus couches this particular prediction in the form of a direct warning. The French did not heed the warning, and hence suffered the predicted disaster.

By 1646, much of the action in the Thirty Years' War was centred in Italy. There was a plot afoot to establish Prince Thomas of Savoy-Carignan as King of Naples, an idea robustly opposed by Pope Innocent X.

The French fleet, under the command of Duke of Breze, assembled at Toulon and sailed to the coast of Tuscany, where they put the French troops ashore. The army besieged Orbetello, a coastal town which faces Corsica and Sardinia. Meanwhile, the French ships encountered the Spanish off Corsica and were defeated. The Duke of Breze was killed during the encounter and the fleet was left in a state of disarray.

THE DEATHS OF RICHELIEU AND LOUIS XIII

The old Cardinal will be deceived by the younger one.
He will find himself disarmed and out of position.
Arles, do not show a double strength perceived,
And both Aqueduct and Prince will be embalmed.

(CENTURY 8 – QUATRAIN 71)

In this quatrain, Nostradamus predicts the rivalry between Cardinal Richelieu – the 'Old Cardinal' – and the twenty-two-year-old Marquis of Cinq-Mars, a favourite of Louis XIII, in 1642. Richelieu was forced to resign and retired to Arles. The Cardinal's secret service, though, soon secured a copy of a treaty with Spain, with whom the French were at war, signed by Cinq-Mars. Richelieu, despite being gravely ill, travelled to Paris by barge – hence 'Aqueduct' – and showed the treasonous document to King Louis XIII. Cinq-Mars was beheaded. The Cardinal died on 4 December, 1642, and Louis the following year. As Nostradamus predicted, both men were embalmed.

THE CHURCH AGAINST THE ASTROLOGERS

**The number of astrologers shall grow so great,
That they will be driven out, banned, and their
books censored
In the year 1607, by the sacred assemblies,
So that none of them shall be safe from the Church.**

(CENTURY 8 – QUATRAIN 71)

As an astrologer of considerable standing and man who had fallen foul of the Church because of his interest in the subject, Nostradamus probably included this quatrain as much as a personal gripe as of a piece of earth-shattering history.

In 1607, Pope Urban VIII banned the influential publication, *Dekkers' Almanac*, under pain of excommunication. This move caused great consternation and merely served to drive the almanac underground.

BRITAIN – PROSPERITY, CIVIL WAR AND DISASTER

While most of Nostradamus's quatrains pertaining to the sixteenth century concentrated on French domestic matters, as he looked further ahead in time, he broadened his geographic scope. The prophet seemed particularly fascinated by the British Isles. His very last quatrain, Century 10 – Quatrain 100, predicts a prosperous and powerful future for the British.

VISION OF AN EMPIRE

**A great empire will arise from England,
Which will be powerful for more than three hundred years.
Large forces of troops will move by land and sea,
To the great discomfort of the Portuguese.**

(CENTURY 10 – QUATRAIN 100)

If many of Nostradamus's prophecies are obscure, this one could not be more straightforward. It is important to remember that, when the prophet penned these lines, England was a minor power on the edge of Europe. It did not seem destined for greatness.

There is a certain amount of controversy about the exact three hundred years to which Nostradamus was referring. Most historians would agree that England's rise to power started during the reign of Elizabeth I, was consolidated in the seventeenth century, and ended after World War II. This is closer to four hundred years than it is to three, but to be fair to Nostradamus he did predict *more* than three hundred years.

The reference to Portugal might appear obscure, but one must remember that, until Britain established itself, Portugal was one of the world's greatest naval powers. This was not a position it would have relinquished with any great pleasure.

CONFLICT WITH SPAIN

**Before the lake where the treasure was cast,
For seven months, its army routed.
The Spaniards will be defeated by the Albions [British]
By delaying giving battle.**

(CENTURY 8 – QUATRAIN 94)

This quatrain is generally thought to refer to the attack on a Spanish fleet in the Bay of Cadiz. Forty Spanish treasure ships, laden with gold from South America, sailed into the bay and dropped anchor after a seven month voyage. Early in the afternoon, Spanish sailors spotted English privateers on the horizon. They were not unduly concerned because they thought it impossible for any navy to mount an attack through the narrow entrance of the bay. They were not in the mood to sail out and confront the English and so retired for a well-earned siesta.

The Spanish, however, had not allowed for the maritime skills of Essex, Raleigh and Howard. The English sailors rode the wind straight into the harbour and mounted a ferocious attack on the Spanish fleet. To prevent the English from getting their hands on the treasure, the Spanish were forced to scupper their entire fleet, forty galleons and thirteen men-of-war, and salvage their gold later.

What is remarkable about this quatrain is not only its clarity, but also the fact that it was written thirty-seven years before the event, when England and Spain were allies.

FLIGHT OF MARY QUEEN OF SCOTS

When a great queen witnesses her own defeat,
She will demonstrate great courage.
Naked and on horseback, she will cross the river,
Pursued by the sword, having outraged her faith.

(CENTURY 1 – QUATRAIN 86)

In this quatrain, Nostradamus describes the flight of Mary Queen of Scots from Scotland. After her defeat at the hands of the Earl of Murray at Carberry Hill, in May 1568, she rode south to England with nothing but the clothes she stood up in. She took a ferry across the River Tweed, but then continued her journey on horseback. She had indeed outraged the church – both Protestant and Catholic – by her relationship with the Earl of Bothwell, supposed killer of her husband, Lord Darnley.

THE CASKET LETTERS

Letters are found in the queen's chest,
They carry no signature and no author's name.
The trick will conceal the offers,
So that they do not know the identity of the lover.

(CENTURY 8 – QUATRAIN 23)

The letters referred to in this quatrain were the property of Mary Queen of Scots. They were supposed to contain information about the death of Lord Darnley, the queen's husband, who was blown up in 1567. They were introduced as evidence before the commissioners in London by the Earl of Morton. The letters vanished in 1584; their authenticity has always been questioned.

THE DEATH OF QUEEN ELIZABETH I

**She who was rejected will return to reign,
Her enemies will become conspirators.
More than ever her rule will be triumphant.
She will die at seventy-three.**

(CENTURY 6 – QUATRAIN 74)

This is a very fair summary of the life and reign of Elizabeth I. She was rejected as a child by her father, Henry VIII, who was hoping for a son and heir. Later, during her reign, she was faced with a series of conspiracies, but she survived them and sustained her position as monarch. It was during her reign that Britain emerged as a major world power, as was predicted by Nostradamus in another quatrain.

Elizabeth was actually seventy years old when she died in 1603, but it is only reasonable to allow Nostradamus a little latitude.

THE FLOODS

**Great Britain, including all of England,
Will experience terrible flooding.
A new league in Italy will make war,
So that they will ally against them.**

(CENTURY 3 – QUATRAIN 70)

What is particularly interesting about this quatrain is the prophet's use of the expression Grande Bretagne. Great Britain did not become an entity until forty years after Nostradamus died, when James I united the thrones of England and Scotland in 1604. In 1607, there were indeed terrible floods in the west country of England, with the area around Bristol being covered for an area of about thirty square miles.

CHARLES I AND PARLIAMENT

A divine wrath will engulf the great Prince,
A short time before his marriage.
Support and credit will suddenly diminish.
Counsel, he will die because of the shaven heads.

(CENTURY 1 – QUATRAIN 88)

In this quatrain, Nostradamus pinpoints the time when Charles I initially incurred the wrath of his Parliament. In 1625, he married Henrietta Maria, a French Catholic princess. At the wedding, Charles decreed that the persecution of Catholics in England should henceforth cease.

Parliament, already enraged by his total disregard for their powers, refused to support this decree and, at the same time, denied his request for funds (credit) for his war against Spain.

Charles governed without a parliament for 11 years. He reintroduced it in 1640 as he was cripplingly short of funds, but by 1642 Civil War had broken out between the King and the Parliamentary faction. After his defeat at the hands of Oliver Cromwell and his Roundheads (shaven heads), he was sentenced to death by his own court (counsel) and was executed in 1649.

From the kingdom of England, an unworthy man is chased;
His counsellor will be burned in anger.
His followers will sink so low,
That the bastard will be almost welcomed.

(CENTURY 3 – QUATRAIN 80)

Nostradamus considered Charles I 'unworthy' because of his undiplomatic attitude towards Parliament, which the prophet considered ill-befitted a monarch.

The counsellor who was burned was Archbishop Laud, executed for treason by Cromwell's men in 1645. A year later, Charles's followers stooped so 'low' as to sell their monarch back to his parliamentary enemies. The 'bastard' alluded to in the last line of the quatrain is probably Charles's nemesis, Oliver Cromwell.

OLIVER CROMWELL

An ambitious colonel engages in intrigue,
And will usurp the great part of the army,
Then mount a false insurrection against his prince.
He will be discovered under his own flag

(CENTURY 4 – QUATRAIN 62)

The ambitious colonel in this quatrain is unquestionably Oliver Cromwell. He did indeed usurp the greater part of Charles I's army and fought with them under the British flag, as opposed to the Royal Standard.

More a butcher than a king,
While born in obscurity, he will achieve empire by force.
Without respect for religion or law, he will bleed the realm.
His day approaches so closely that I sigh.

(CENTURY 8 – QUATRAIN 76)

Despite the fact that Cromwell was not born until thirty years after his own death, Nostradamus took a ready dislike to him. Although Cromwell eventually established himself as an absolute ruler, the prophet considered him 'more a butcher than a king' because of the bloody excesses of the Civil War.

Cromwell was of humble origins and Nostradamus, a firm royalist, considered that only the aristocracy had the right to rule. Cromwell was also a Protestant, which, in the prophet's eyes, made him a heretic.

By those with shaven heads he will be wrongly elected.
Bowed down by a load that he is unable to carry,
Such great rage and fury will he exhibit,
That to fire and blood all sex will be reduced.

(CENTURY 5 – QUATRAIN 60)

The Parliamentarians – 'shaven heads' – wore their hair much shorter than the dandified Royalists and it was they who elected Cromwell as their leader, despite the fact that there was a king on the throne who ruled by divine right.

The last two lines of the quatrain have been interpreted in a number of ways; perhaps the most convincing is that Nostradamus is suggesting that the Puritans sublimated their sexuality in favour of violence. This is a very modern psychological concept, but it must be remembered that Nostradamus was not confined by the limits of his own time.

CIVIL WAR

A great orator, bold and shameless,
Will gain control of the great army.
The force of his contention,
The broken bridge, the city faint from fear.

(CENTURY 3 – QUATRAIN 81)

The orator in this quatrain is again Oliver Cromwell, who indeed gained control of the army. The last line of the verse is particularly interesting and is a typical example of Nostradamus's use of puns and classical references. In Latin, broken bridge translates as *pons fractus* and here it is a pun for Pontefract, where Charles I and his army had a stronghold. Cromwell besieged Pontefract twice during the Civil War.

THE ARREST OF CHARLES I

**The fortress beside the Thames,
Will fall when the king is jailed inside.
He will be seen in his shirt near the bridge,
One facing death then barred inside the fortress.**

(CENTURY 8 – QUATRAIN 37)

This is another of Nostradamus's triumphs of prophecy. Following his defeat and capture in 1647, Charles I was for a while incarcerated in Hampton Court, and much later in Windsor Castle, either of which might be 'The fortress beside the Thames'. On 30 January 1649, after his trial, he was led to the scaffold in Whitehall, dressed in a white shirt and no jacket, and was beheaded. Later, his blood-stained shirt was hung from a pole on London Bridge as a warning to other Royalists.

THE EUROPEAN PLOT

Ghent and Brussels march against Antwerp.
The Parliament of London put their king to death.
The salt and wine oppose him.
On account of their actions, the kingdom will be in disarray.

(CENTURY 9 – QUATRAIN 49)

Despite his defeat at the hands of the Parliamentarians, Charles I continued to plot. In 1648, the Thirty Years' War in Europe had just ended, and the continent was swimming with unemployed soldiers. Many of his supporters had already been exiled to mainland Europe and they started recruiting on his behalf. The plot came to naught, because Charles was tried and beheaded before an army could be mustered. It is for this reason that Nostradamus set this quatrain about the execution of Charles I in a European context.

The last two lines of the quatrain portray the kingdom as being in a state of disarray. This, too, was prophetic. The execution of the King achieved nothing and Britain was soon plunged into even greater turmoil.

THE BATTLE OF WORCESTER

At midnight, the leader of the army
Will run away, disappearing completely.
Seven years later, his reputation unsullied,
He will return, and to this 'yes' shall be said and not once.

(CENTURY 10 – QUATRAIN 46)

In 1651, just over two years after the execution of Charles I and the establishment of a republic, or Commonwealth, as it was known, the rightful heir to the throne, Charles II, raised an army to recapture his kingdom. He was defeated by Cromwell's army at the Battle of Worcester and fled in disguise first to Scotland, and thence to France.

As Nostradamus predicted, Cromwell effectively ruled Britain as a despot for another seven years. When he died in 1658, his eldest son, Richard, was proclaimed Lord Protector of England. Richard had little interest or ability in politics, and the following year was effectively deposed by the army. In 1660, Charles II was recalled from exile and restored to the throne.

THE GREAT PLAGUE

A just man will wrongfully be put to death,
Publicly and in the midst of a crowd, he will be killed.
So great a plague will arise in that place,
That his executioners will be forced to flee.

(CENTURY 9 – QUATRAIN 11)

In the sixteenth century, royalty were still considered to have magical abilities. A touch from a king was supposed to cure all manner of ills. It is not surprising, therefore, that an avowed royalist like Nostradamus should believe that the killing of a king might unleash a plague on those responsible for his death.

However, it was not until five years after Charles II became king, and sixteen years after Charles I was beheaded, that the Great Plague swept through London, killing more than 70,000 men, women and children.

The great plague in a maritime city,
Will not cease until the death is avenged
Of one just man, condemned without crime.
The great lady is outraged by the hypocrisy.

(CENTURY 2 – QUATRAIN 53)

In this second quatrain predicting the Great Plague, Nostradamus repeats his assertion that the epidemic was God's retribution for the execution of Charles I. The 'great lady' in the last line of the quatrain is generally considered to be a metaphor for the Catholic Church, 'outraged' by the rise of Protestanism throughout Britain.

THE GREAT FIRE OF LONDON

The blood of the just man will be demanded from London,
Burnt in fire in three times twenty and six.
The old lady will fall from her place on high,
And many of the same religion will be killed.

(CENTURY 2 – QUATRAIN 51)

Nostradamus obviously considered that the Great Plague was insufficient retribution for the execution of Charles I, and he prophesied that the people of London would have to pay an even higher price for their sins. This would take the form of the Great Fire of London, which raged for four days in 1666.

The quatrain is very detailed. The old lady – *dame antique* – in the third line is generally considered to be St. Paul's Cathedral, which was destroyed in the fire, along with 89 parish churches.

There were, however, very few deaths during the fire, and several of these were due to opportunistic murders.

WILLIAM OF ORANGE & JAMES II

**Thirty Londoners will plot against their king,
The deed will take place at sea.
The reality of his father's death appals him.
A fair haired king from Friesland will be chosen.**

(CENTURY 4 – QUATRAIN 89)

The *Centuries* contain several quatrains which predict the defeat of the House of Stuart by William of Orange.

When he ascended the throne on the death of his father, Charles II, in 1685, King James II knew that he faced real problems both on the political and religious fronts. When his son and heir, Prince James Edward, was born in 1688 and baptised a Catholic, public hostility towards the monarchy reached crisis point.

On 30 June, ten days after the prince's birth, Admiral Arthur Herbert went to Friesland, in the Netherlands, for an audience with the

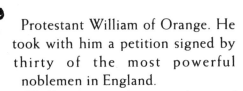

Protestant William of Orange. He took with him a petition signed by thirty of the most powerful noblemen in England.

William was the grandson of Charles I, on his mother's side, and was married to James II's daughter, Mary. He therefore considered himself to have a legitimate claim to the English throne, and accepted Herbert's invitation to lead a revolution against his father-in-law.

On November 5 1688, William of Orange landed at Torbay; seven weeks later, James II conceded defeat and fled to France. On 23 February 1689, Parliament passed the Bill of Rights, which, amongst other things, determined the succession to the crown. Under this new legislation, William and Mary were established as joint monarchs, and from that day on, all Catholics were precluded from the English throne.

The blond man will fight the one with a hooked nose.
He will drive him out in a battle.
Exiles will be restored,
The strongest of whom will be assigned to the maritime.

(CENTURY 2 – QUATRAIN 67)

In Century 2, Nostradamus presents three consecutive quatrains, 67-69, on a single topic, the fight for the British throne between James II and William of Orange. This is rare. Generally, individual quatrains on any given subject or person are scattered randomly through the various volumes.

In quatrain 67, the 'blond man' is William of Orange and the 'one with a hooked nose' is James II. After William took the

English throne in 1688, the Stuart party attempted to reinstate James, who established a base in Catholic Ireland and recruited the French navy to his cause. The combined forces had a notable victory off Beachy Head on 30 June 1690, but the following day William defeated the Stuart army at the Battle of the Boyne in the north of Ireland. James II was forced to flee to France, where he remained until his death.

The British fleet did not, however, gain supremacy over the French until the battle at Cap du Hague, two years later.

> **The efforts in the north shall be great;**
> **Across the seas there will be an opportunity.**
> **Rule on the island will be restored;**
> **London shall be intimidated by the fleet.**

(CENTURY 2 – QUATRAIN 68)

The 'efforts in the north' in this quatrain refers to William of Orange's campaign against the Stuarts in northern Ireland. The combined Stuart and French navies were having considerable success at sea, notably at Beachy Head and Bantry Bay, and it was only William's strength on land that enabled him to retain power.

The island referred to in the third line of the quatrain is Ireland, where James II had indeed re-established his rule, until his defeat at the Battle of the Boyne on 12 July 1690.

The last line refers to the succession of British defeats

at sea. The fleet was ineffectively commanded by Lord Torrington who, after the defeat at Beachy Head, was recalled to London and court-martialled.

> The Gallic king from the Celtic right,
> Seeing discord in the great monarchy,
> Will brandish his sceptre over the three leopards,
> Against the king of the great hierarchy.

(CENTURY 2 – QUATRAIN 69)

In this final quatrain in the William of Orange/James II sequence, the Gallic king is William, who took over the throne of England from James II, not by battle but by invitation from noblemen seeking a Protestant king.

The 'leopards' in the third line are thought to refer to the English heraldic lions.

ANOTHER VISION OF BRITAIN

> Seven changes will be seen within the British Nation,
> Soaked in blood for two hundred and ninety years.
> France is untouched by Germany's influence.
> Aries fears for the security of Poland.

(CENTURY 3 – QUATRAIN 57)

This quatrain, the second dealing with Britain's long-term future, is an intriguing conundrum. The main problem is to decide from which point in time the two hundred and ninety years should be calculated, and which seven specific changes are being alluded to.

Most commentators begin in the sixteenth century, either with the Reformation under Henry VIII or the increase in maritime power under Elizabeth I. However, beginning with the execution of Charles I in 1649, 290 years takes us to the beginning of World War II, sparked off by a threat to 'the security of Poland'.

C H A P T E R   3

THE FRENCH
REVOLUTION

Nostradamus predicted the civil unrest in France in the eighteenth century, and the Revolution which stemmed from it. No other episode in history generated more quatrains, and they enabled the reader to preview the events with remarkable accuracy.

When the litters are overturned by the whirlwind,
And their faces are hidden by their cloaks,
The Republic will be troubled by the revolutionaries,
As both whites and reds will be equally mistaken in
their judgment.

(CENTURY 1 – QUATRAIN 3)

This quatrain is the first of dozens of prophecies by Nostradamus concerning the French Revolution. It is also one of the most lucid.

Litters were a mode of transport favoured by the French aristocracy, and the image of them being overturned is a metaphor for the overthrow of the monarchy. The word 'whirlwind' is one much favoured by the prophet when describing the Revolution. The expression 'faces hidden by their cloaks' could refer to members of the aristocracy who fled the country in disguise, or possibly to the heads that fell from the guillotine and were then hidden from sight.

In the next line, Nostradamus refers to France as a republic, an unthinkable concept in his own time, and diametrically opposed to his own heartfelt royalist sympathies. The significance of 'reds' and 'whites' in the last line of the quatrain could not be simpler. The Bourbons' emblem was a white cockade, while red was the colour adopted by the revolutionaries.

Ancient traditions which served as the strength of the
people shall be denounced,
And the people shall rise up against the king.
A brief truce shall be declared, and the holy laws destroyed.
Never was Paris in such a terrible situation.

(CENTURY 6 – QUATRAIN 23)

This is very general quatrain predicting the French Revolution.
The 'ancient traditions' were indeed denounced by the masses,
who were determined to bring down the monarchy. There was a
brief truce in· 1791, but the whole thing flared up again and things
in the capital were perhaps at their very worst.

From an enslaved people come songs, chants and demands.
The Princes and Lords are held captive in prison:
In the future by headless idiots,
These will be taken as divine utterances.

(CENTURY 1 – QUATRAIN 14)

In this quatrain, Nostradamus presents a picture of the
revolutionaries as a mob, marching through the capital, protest-
ing, chanting and singing the Marseillaise. While horrified by
the idea of a republic, the prophet does seem to concede that
the common man has some genuine grievance against the
status quo when he describes them as 'an enslaved
people'. The use of the term 'headless idiots' is a
typical Nostradamus pun, referring both to a
lack of political intelligence and the fate of many
at the hands of Madame Guillotine.

Under the pretext of freeing the people
The people themselves will usurp power.
He shall do worse because of the trickery of a young whore.
He shall betray in the field, delivering a false promise.

(CENTURY 5 – QUATRAIN 5)

In this quatrain, Nostradamus paints a very general picture of the French Revolution. He was correct to say that the regime which replaced the deposed Louis XVI was equally repressive.

The 'young whore' is Marie Antoinette, who was wildly unpopular because of her extravagance in a time of terrible poverty. Her popularity further diminished after the 'Diamond Necklace Affair', a complicated scandal which broke in 1785; it was suggested that the queen was having an affair with a cardinal.

The 'false promise' in the last line of the quatrain probably refers to Louis XVI's promise not to leave the Tuileries, where he and his family had been incarcerated for their own protection. He broke this promise and attempted to flee the country in June 1791, but was captured at Varennes.

THE STORMING OF THE BASTILLE

Before the war, the great wall will fall
The King will be executed, his death very sudden, and
lamented.
The masses will swim in blood,
And near the Seine, the soil will be bloodstained.

(CENTURY 2 – QUATRAIN 57)

According to a contemporary report, the masses had assembled at
the Bastille on 14 July 1789 with the intention of demonstrating,
but the walls were so poorly defended that they soon fell. De
Launay, the Governor of the Bastille, was murdered by the mob.

THE NATIONAL ASSEMBLY

The topography shall be changed completely,
The urns in the tombs shall be opened.
Philosophy shall usurp religion.
Black will pass for white, novelties for tradition.

(CENTURY 7 – QUATRAIN 14)

In this quatrain, Nostradamus predicts the events of 22 December 1789, when the National Assembly radically changed the map of France. They replaced the ancient regions with a series of *départements*. At about the same time, the tombs of the Kings of France at St Denis were being desecrated, and their ashes scattered to the winds.

In the last two lines, Nostradamus appears to be saying nothing more profound than that the entire value structure of the French nation was going to be stood on its head.

ROBESPIERRE AND THE REIGN OF TERROR

He who has already established some power,
Having red ideas, will reach the top of the hierarchy.
Stubborn and cruel, he will make himself terribly feared,
And will succeed to the consecrated monarchy.

(CENTURY 6 – QUATRAIN 57)

This quatrain refers to Maximilien Robespierre and his excesses. In June 1791, Robespierre, a lawyer, was appointed Public Prosecutor for the Criminal Tribunal of the Seine. He allied himself with the Jacobins, the extreme wing of the French revolutionaries, and in 1792 was elected to the National Convention, which proclaimed the Republic.

He led the prosecution in the trial of King Louis XVI and lobbied vehemently for the death penalty.

Robespierre established the Revolutionary Tribunal and, following the execution of the king in January 1793, launched the Reign of Terror. He proceeded to subject the people of France to a blood-thirsty, tyrannical regime in which nobody was safe from the guillotine. Finally, those colleagues who had survived, tired of his arrogant extremism, conspired against him.

> The fox will be elected without uttering a word,
> Playing the public saint and living on bread.
> Afterwards he will turn into a tyrant,
> Placing his foot on the throats of the greatest.

(CENTURY 8 – QUATRAIN 41)

Robespierre's cunning and deviousness earned him the nick-name of 'the fox'. By 1793, having eliminated all effective opposition in the Assembly, he had secured himself the position of a virtual dictator of France.

Robespierre played the public saint and was proud of his austere and puritanical life style. As Nostradamus predicted, he did turn into a tyrant. At the height of his powers, he declared that 'Any individual who usurps the nation's sovereignty will immediately be put to death by free men.' The Reign of Terror was born.

Without support, the Capet family will be disturbed.
The Reds will march in order to consolidate it.
A royal family will be virtually consumed by death.
The Red extremists will destroy the Red one and his
followers.

(CENTURY 8 – QUATRAIN 19)

After the execution of Louis XVI, Marie-Antoinette and Princess
Elizabeth, and the death of Louis XVII in prison, the French royal
family, named here after an earlier dynasty, the House of Capet,
was indeed virtually wiped out.

The 'Red one' undoubtedly refers to Robespierre (ruby stone).
Once the hero of the Revolution, he soon fell out of favour. He
was considered to be proud, stubborn and fanatical. Soon there
was a conspiracy within his own ranks to get rid of him. He was
arrested on 27 July 1794 and guillotined, along with twenty-two
of his supporters, the following day. The Great Terror ended in
mass slaughter.

THE DEATH OF ROBESPIERRE

The cock, the cats and dogs will have had their fill of blood,
When the tyrant is found dying of a wound in a strange bed.
Both arms and legs will be broken,
And he who is not afraid dies a terrible death

(CENTURY 2 – QUATRAIN 42)

The cock is the emblem of France, and the dogs and cats appear to describe the French masses. Both had had enough of the bloodletting during Robespierre's Reign of Terror – more than a thousand executions in the space of a fortnight – and vowed to topple him.

On 26 July 1794, Robespierre was arrested but was freed almost immediately by his supporters. That night, he stayed in the Hôtel de Ville – 'a strange bed' – but he was recaptured by the National Guard the following day. He was shot in the jaw during the arrest – not in the arms and legs as Nostradamus suggests. Robespierre was executed, without trial, at the Place de la Révolution later that day.

THE THIRD ESTATE

The government, usurped by the Third, will be barbarous,
And will put to death innumerable of its own people.
The fourth man, senile, struck dead by his country,
Fears lest his blood line might end.

(CENTURY 3 – QUATRAIN 59)

This quatrain clearly describes aspects of the French Revolution but is quite obscure. The first two lines are fairly straightforward, referring to the victory of the 'Third Estate'. Erika Cheetham suggests the 'fourth man' might be Napoleon, the first three being the three Committees of Public Safety – the ruling bodies in revolutionary France – namely those of Danton, Robespierre and

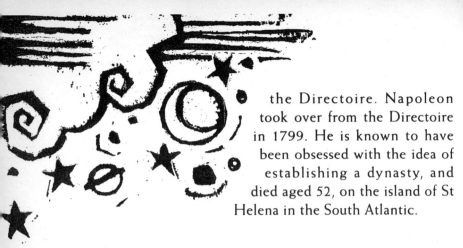

the Directoire. Napoleon took over from the Directoire in 1799. He is known to have been obsessed with the idea of establishing a dynasty, and died aged 52, on the island of St Helena in the South Atlantic.

Soon everything will be organised.
We anticipate an evil century.
The condition of the masked and solitary much changed,
Few will find that they wish to retain their rank.

(CENTURY 2 – QUATRAIN 10)

In this quatrain, Nostradamus predicts the demolition of two specific social orders during the French Revolution. The first – 'the masked' – was the monarchy and the aristocracy; the second – 'the solitary' – was the Church. Many aristocrats and churchmen were stripped of their assets. Others faced the ultimate sanction of the guillotine. It is hardly surprising, therefore, that few were prepared to acknowledge, let alone adhere to, the rank they held under the old order.

The third one finally does worse than Nero.
Go flow brave human blood;
The furnace will be rebuilt.
A golden century, then death, a new king and a scandal.

(Century 9 – Quatrain 17)

The 'third' refers to the Third Estate – that is, the people in general, rather than the aristocracy and clergy – in Revolutionary France, which Nostradamus predicts will be more brutal than Nero, the debauched and cruel Roman emperor. Blood, he says, will flow freely from the guillotines. These were erected in the Place de la Révolution, which previously housed the furnaces of a tile company.

The last line laments the passing of the golden century of Louis XIV and Louix XV, who ruled for 130 years. Then came Louis XVI and the 'scandal' of the Revolution.

LOUIS XVI AND MARIE ANTOINETTE

JUDGMENT AND RETRIBUTION

In a good age, the king is also good.
He will be killed promptly because of negligence.
The kings's wife shall be wrongly accused of being licentious,
And she shall be put to death because of her nature.

(CENTURY 10 – QUATRAIN 43)

At the end of the eighteenth century, France was one of richest and most advanced countries in the world, and in some ways Louis XVI was a good king. He appointed some far-sighted ministers who, sensing the public unrest, started to bring about reforms. However, the King had carried on the tradition of borrowing heavily from the exchequer and failing to pay it back – 'negligence'. Much of this money was squandered to finance Marie Antoinette's extravagant lifestyle. This, together with her arrogant attitude towards the people, made her deeply unpopular and eventually led her to the guillotine.

Too much of a good time and too much royal bounty,
Made and undone by sudden negligence.
He will readily believe his false wife to be loyal,
Whom in his benevolence he puts to death.

(CENTURY 10 – QUATRAIN 43)

Louis XVI's downfall came in part from his irresponsibility and dereliction of duty. Marie Antoinette was a greedy and manipulative woman who took advantage of her husband's weak character and thereby contributed greatly to his eventual execution.

THE FLIGHT TO VARENNES

By night there will come by the forest of Reines
A married couple, by a devious route.
A Queen – white stone, a monk-king in grey at Varennes.
Elected Capet, causes tempest, fire and bloody slicing.

(CENTURY 9 – QUATRAIN 20)

This is perhaps one of Nostradamus' most impressive quatrains. It describes the royal family's escape from the Tuileries and attempt to flee the country. Their road to freedom took them through the forest of Reines. They were heading for a hiding place in Varennes but their coachman lost his way and took a 'devious' route.

The 'Queen – white stone' obviously refers to Marie Antoinette and is apt for a number of reasons. On the night of her escape, she

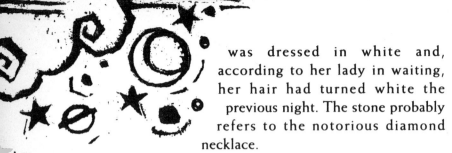

was dressed in white and, according to her lady in waiting, her hair had turned white the previous night. The stone probably refers to the notorious diamond necklace.

King Louis XVI was wearing all grey when he entered Varennes. He was a Capet – and elected monarch – and he did indeed bring about 'tempest, fire and bloody slicing'.

The partner, alone but married, will wear a mitre.
The return, fighting will break out to the Tuileries:
By five hundred, one traitor will be ennobled.
Narbonne and Saulce will have oil for knives.

(CENTURY 9 – QUATRAIN 34)

This quatrain shows Nostradamus at the height of his powers. When King Louis XVI and Marie Antoinette reached Varennes, they spent a night at the home of the Saulce family. The Saulces have been chandlers in the city since the sixteenth century.

The reference to the King wearing a mitre refers to his return to the Tuileries on 20 June 1792. When the mob invaded the palace, they forced the King to wear a revolutionary cap, which bore a strong resemblance to a mitre. A contemporary report stated that the invaders numbered exactly five hundred.

THE TRIAL AND EXECUTION OF LOUIS XVI

Great discord shakes the land,
An agreement having been broken. His head lifted
to the heavens,
His bloody mouth shall swim with blood;
His face, anointed with milk and honey, shall lie
on the ground.

(CENTURY 1 – QUATRAIN 57)

This is one of the few quatrains upon which interpreters of Nostradamus are almost universally agreed. It refers to the execution of King Louis XVI on 21 January, 1793. The time of 'great discord' in the first line refers to the broken constitutional agreement between the King and the National Assembly.

According to contemporary reports, as the King climbed onto the scaffold, he raised his eyes to the heavens and recited the third verse of the Third Psalm - 'But thou, O Lord, art a shield for me; my glory, and the lifter up of mine head.' Then the guillotine blade fell and blood spewed from the King's mouth. His head – which had been anointed with milk and honey on the day of his coronation – lay severed on the ground.

Blood will be shed before the people,
And he will not be far from heaven.
For a long time he will no longer be understood,
Until the spirit of one who comes one day to bear witness.

(CENTURY 4 – QUATRAIN 49)

As Louis XVI was led from the tumbrel to the guillotine, he is reported to have cried out, 'People, I die innocent!' In his will, however, after forgiving his enemies and urging his son to do likewise, he ended by declaring to God that he was ready to appear before him.

In the last two lines of the quatrain, Nostradamus suggests that the fate of Louis's son, the Dauphin, known as but never crowned Louis XVII, would remain a mystery until one of his descendants uncovered the truth.

It will be wrong to put a man to death and execute him
before his people.
It will bring upon this spot such a great calamity,
That those who did not vote
Will be condemned to flee.

(CENTURY 9 – QUATRAIN 11)

In this quatrain, Nostradamus condemns the execution of the king and rightly predicts that it would unleash the Reign of Terror. In the last two lines, the prophet correctly assumes that anyone who did not vote for the execution would be forced to flee from Paris.

MARIE ANTOINETTE IMPRISONED

**The Queen, detained like a slave, seeing her
daughter waste away
Will regret that she had children,
Swayed by the lamentations of the Duchess of Angoulême,
Married to her first cousin in an unholy union.**

(CENTURY 10 – QUATRAIN 17)

During her imprisonment in the Temple, Marie Antoinette suffered every form of hardship and humiliation imaginable. Early in 1793, she was joined in prison by her daughter, Marie-Thérèse. Marie-Thérèse later married her first cousin, the Duke of Angoulême, son of the Count d'Artois, her father's younger brother, and the future King Charles X.

EXECUTION OF MARIE ANTOINETTE

**The kingdom taken, the Queen sent to her death
By jurors chosen by lot.
They will deny the Queen's son,
And the whore shares the fate of the consort.**

(CENTURY 9 – QUATRAIN 77)

Nine months after the execution of her husband, Marie Antoinette followed him to the guillotine. Nostradamus's prediction in this quatrain is very accurate, even down the point that the jurors for her trial were chosen by lot.

The fate of Marie Antoinette's son, who should have become King, remains one of the mysteries of the period. Young Louis, born in 1785, was taken from his mother and lodged in the Temple prison, where he was placed in the care of a cobbler named Simon. Simon was instructed to humble his ward. It is widely believed that the young prince died as the direct result of physical abuse.

The whore referred to in the last line of the quatrain is undoubtedly Madame du Barry, the long-time mistress of Louis XV, and Marie Antoinette's arch rival at court. As Nostradamus predicted, she followed the queen to the guillotine.

THE PERSECUTION OF THE CLERGY

A great tragedy will occur not long after:
Those who once gave will be forced to receive.
Naked, starving, cold and thirsty, they will band together,
And cross the mountains, causing a great scandal.

(CENTURY 6 – QUATRAIN 69)

In 1792, France declared the disestablishment of the Church, and many priests, robbed of their living, were forced to endure great hardship. Where once they had been in the position to dole out alms, now they were forced to beg to survive. Many of them fled from France across the Alps, and their plight caused a great scandal with French Christians.

> Blood will pour from the bodies of churchmen,
> It will be as abundant as water.
> For a long time it will not be restrained.
> Woe, woe for the clergy, ruin and grief.

(CENTURY 8 – QUATRAIN 98)

Here again Nostradamus bemoans the fate of the clergy in the wake of the disestablishment of the Church.

THE CULT OF REASON

> In a short time sacrifices will resume.
> Those oppressed will be put to death like martyrs.
> There will no longer be monks, abbots or novices.
> Honey shall be more expensive than wax.

(CENTURY 1 – QUATRAIN 44)

On 10 November, 1793, the French Revolutionary government announced the Cult of Reason which abolished the worship of God. To this end, the Constitution declared the abolition of the clergy. Many refused to abandon Christianity and were persecuted for their beliefs.

The last line in the quatrain refers to the price of beeswax, which had hitherto been extremely expensive and in great demand for the manufacture of votive candles. With the abolition of the Church, however, the price dropped dramatically until it was less expensive than honey.

THE WHITE TERROR

**The Chouan army will rise up against the Montagnards,
Who, being warned, will trap it.
They will push back the peasants with ease,
Forcing them into the marshes, and killing them.**

(CENTURY 4 – QUATRAIN 63)

As Nostradamus predicted, France was thrown into a state of bloody chaos after the execution of Louis XVI. The prophet foresaw two of the more spectacular events in these early days of the Republic.

In this quatrain, he describes a battle in Brittany in 1795 between the Chouans, anti-Republican rebels supported by the British, and the Republican army. The Chouans were soundly defeated and retreated to the marshlands where they were virtually wiped out. Some survivors of the battle were later executed.

THE MASSACRE AT NANTES

Some of the leading citizens of the rebellious city,
Will try to regain their liberty.
The men are cut up, unhappy confusion;
Cries and wails at Nantes will be pitiful to see.

(CENTURY 5 – QUATRAIN 33)

During the early days of the Revolution, the city of Nantes was the scene of several atrocities. In 1793, many of its leading citizens allied themselves with neighbouring districts and formed an organisation called the Central Assembly of Resistance to Oppression. The National Convention got wind of this, and the response was as swift as it was brutal. In 1793, more than 1,000 citizens of Nantes were put to death. The majority were guillotined, but some were tied up and thrown into the River Loire to drown.

CHAPTER 4

NAPOLEON – THE FIRST ANTICHRIST

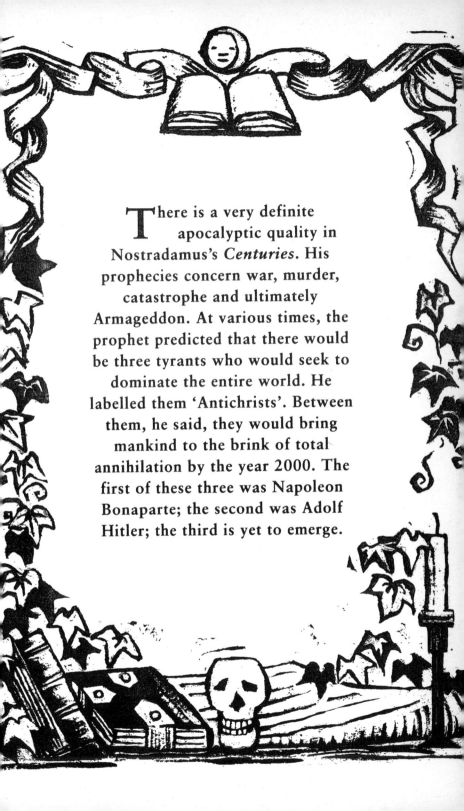

There is a very definite apocalyptic quality in Nostradamus's *Centuries*. His prophecies concern war, murder, catastrophe and ultimately Armageddon. At various times, the prophet predicted that there would be three tyrants who would seek to dominate the entire world. He labelled them 'Antichrists'. Between them, he said, they would bring mankind to the brink of total annihilation by the year 2000. The first of these three was Napoleon Bonaparte; the second was Adolf Hitler; the third is yet to emerge.

As with the French Revolution, Nostradamus is both prolific and astonishingly accurate in tracing the dictator's progress through history, from his humble beginnings as a young Corsican artillery lieutenant, through his rise to absolute dictator of the majority of mainland Europe, and on to his defeat, exile and death.

THE BIRTH OF AN EMPEROR

An Emperor will be born near Italy,
Who will cost his empire dearly.
They will say when they see his allies,
That he is less a prince than a butcher.

(CENTURY 1 – QUATRAIN 60)

This is perhaps one of Nostradamus most famous quatrains. Napoleon was born in Corsica in 1769. The island had been bought by Louis XV of France two years earlier from Italy. It was therefore no longer Italian, but was not, as yet, officially part of France. Hence Nostradamus's description of 'near Italy' refers not only to Corsica's geographical location, but also its political status.

Nostradamus goes on to say that the 'Emperor' will 'cost his empire dearly'. Ultimately this proved to be true. After Napoleon's defeat and exile in 1815, all the territorial gains he had achieved were eradicated and he left France a weaker country than the one he had inherited. He also cost the empire dearly in terms of lives lost. Almost twenty per cent of the adult male population of the country were killed in the Napoleonic wars.

The last line of the quatrain, where Nostradamus describes Napoleon as more a butcher than a prince, is almost identical to his assessment of Oliver Cromwell.

> **He will be known by a barbaric name,**
> **Which shall be derived from those of the three fates.**
> **He will speak great words and do great deeds,**
> **And more than anyone he will gain fame and renown.**

(CENTURY 1 – QUATRAIN 76)

The most interesting aspect of this quatrain is not its content, but rather Nostradamus's play on words. The 'barbaric' name Napoleon derives from two Greek words, *nea*, meaning new, and *polluon*, meaning exterminator. Thus Napoleon was the new exterminator.

As Nostradamus points out in the third line, Napoleon was not only a great strategist, he was also a great orator. His pre-battle speeches were legendary and widely credited with having inspired his men to defeat numerically superior forces.

RISE TO POWER

From a simple soldier he will seize an Empire.
His short robe shall be exchanged for long.
Brave in arms and much worse towards the Church,
He vexes priests as water fills a sponge.

(CENTURY 8 – QUATRAIN 57)

In this quatrain, Nostradamus gives us a thumb-nail sketch of Napoleon's rise to power from a 'simple soldier'. He gave up the short robe or tunic of a consul for the long, flowing robes of an emperor.

Nostradamus was right to call Napoleon 'brave at arms', but he was equally correct in his description of Bonaparte's appalling treatment of the clergy.

ITALY AND EGYPT

TOULON

From the marine and tributary city,
The crophead will take his seat of government,
To chase the sordid men who are against him.
For fourteen years he will exercise his tyranny.

(CENTURY 7 – QUATRAIN 13)

This quatrain refers to Napoleon's first spectacular military success. In 1793, still only a lieutenant, the twenty-four year old Napoleon took command of the French forces at Toulon, where he defeated the English.

Much later, when he entered politics, Napoleon cut his hair very short and brushed it forward in the fashion of his hero, Julius Caesar. He then went on to overthrow the Directoire – 'the sordid men' – in 1799. He continued to hold on to power until 1814, a few months longer than Nostradamus predicted.

The Italian lands near the mountains will quake.
The cock and the lion are not comfortably united.
They will help each other out of fear.
Freedom alone moderates the French.

(CENTURY 1 – QUATRAIN 93)

In 1795, after his victory at Toulon, Napoleon embarked upon his Italian campaign. Victory followed victory, but the French, symbolised by a cock, were becoming increasingly uneasy about a threat from the English 'lion'. The English were likewise concerned about France's expansionist ambitions. For this reason, the two countries entered a brief and uneasy alliance.

VILLA NOVA

At the New City he considers attack;
The bird of prey offers himself to the gods.
After victory he pardons his captives.
At Cremona and Mantua great hardships shall be endured.

(CENTURY 1 – QUATRAIN 24)

Early in his Italian campaign, in 1796, Napoleon reached Villa Nova – 'New City' – and was unsure how to proceed. He had no orders to attack from the Directoire, and so continued on to Mantua, which he besieged. Despite heavy bombardment, the city held out for more than seven months before finally surrendering. Napoleon, 'the bird of prey', respected the citizens' courage, and is said to have treated them very fairly. Two years later, however, Mantua and its neighbour, Cremona, were taken by the Austrians and subjected to terrible persecution.

MILAN

Before the attack a speech is delivered.
Milan, fooled by an ambush, is captured by the Eagle.
The ancient walls are breached by cannon.
In fire and blood, few receive quarter.

(CENTURY 3 – QUATRAIN 37)

When Napoleon took over France's Italian Army, it was in a terrible state. The troops had no cold-weather clothing, precious little equipment and were ill-trained and in low spirits. His powers of oratory alone are credited for imbuing them with the will to fight and the tenacity to win.

In this quatrain, Nostradamus is describing Napoleon's occupation of Milan on 15 May, 1796. He went on to take the city for a second time in 1800, during his subsequent Italian campaign.

FROM ITALY TO EGYPT

The great Po will suffer great hardship from a Frenchman.
Great terror to the maritime Lion.
Vast numbers of people will cross the sea,
And a quarter of a million will perish.

(CENTURY 2 – QUATRAIN 94)

This quatrain marks the transition period between Napoleon's Italian and Egyptian campaigns. He had already inflicted considerable damage in Italy and this was of great concern to England, 'the maritime Lion'.

As Nostradamus predicted, Napoleon did take his great army across the sea to Egypt and at least a quarter of a million men on all sides died during his campaigns.

DEFEAT AT SEA

The fleet will be wrecked near the Adriatic sea.
The earth trembles, rises into the air and falls again.
Egypt quakes; the power of the Mahometan increases;
The herald is sent out to call for surrender.

(CENTURY 2 – QUATRAIN 86)

In 1798, the French and British Fleets met in the Battle of the Nile. The French were thoroughly trounced. The second line of this quatrain refers to the French army who, having disembarked, were terrified when they heard that the admiral's flag ship had been blown up and scattered along the beach.

After his defeat at sea, Napoleon led his troops against the Turks – 'Mahometan'. He besieged the port of Acre, but after two months, the French army was stricken with a plague and Napoleon was forced to withdraw to Egypt. They engaged the Turks again but were unable to break down their resistance. In an act of bravado, Napoleon sent out a messenger and demanded a Turkish surrender. This was refused and Napoleon was obliged to abandon his campaign.

THE BIRTH OF AN EMPIRE

COUP D'ETAT

A great swarm of bees will rise,
But no one will know from where they came:
The ambush by night; the jay will settle himself in
the trellises.
The city will be betrayed by five corrupt babblers.

(CENTURY 4 – QUATRAIN 26)

This is perhaps the most dense quatrain dealing with the Napoleonic era. It refers to the coup d'état of 9 November 1799, which overthrew the Directoire and established Napoleon as one of three 'consuls' – the other two were figureheads – governing France.

The 'swarm of bees' was one of Napoleon's emblems. Bees can still be seen at Malmaison and Fontainebleau – both decorated by the Emperor – where they adorn the carpets, wall hangings and even the silk backs to the chairs.

The ambush is the coup d'état itself, which was

planned the previous night and was a complete success. Napoleon installed himself in the Tuileries. Like the jay in the quatrain, he decked himself out in peacock feathers to emulate the splendour of the ancient Kings of France.

The 'five corrupt babblers' are the executive counsellors of the Directoire; two of them conspired directly with Napoleon, while the other three were bribed to look the other way.

THE FIRST CONSUL

The miserable, unfortunate Republic
Will be devastated by a new Magistrate.
The great number of exiles causing trouble
Will make the Germans withdraw their alliance.

(CENTURY 1 – QUATRAIN 61)

Shortly after his coup d'état, Napoleon presented a new constitution under which he held the casting vote. As First Consul, he had the sole power of decision, and furthermore he held the right to propose legislation. He was, in effect, a dictator from that moment on.

The alliance with the Germans, referred to in the last two lines of the quatrain, lasted in various shaky forms until 1813, when Prussia sided with Russia. Austria declared herself against France and Napoleon in the same year, and her example was quickly followed by Bavaria, Württemburg and Saxony.

THE BATTLE OF TRAFALGAR

With corvettes and frigates around seven ships,
A deadly battle will take place.
The Spanish leader will be wounded.
Two ships which escape will be led back by five others.

(CENTURY 7 – QUATRAIN 26)

In predicting the battle of Trafalgar, Nostradamus is once again impressive in his detail. At 7 a.m. on 21 October 1805, the Franco-Spanish fleet, consisting of thirty-three warships and seven frigates, was at anchor when Nelson's fleet was seen approaching. The battle of Trafalgar raged for almost twelve hours and left the Franco-Spanish fleet wrecked. Rear-Admiral Magon and the Spanish Admiral Gravina were both killed during the battle, as indeed was Horatio Nelson.

TRAFALGAR

A promontory stands between two seas.
A man will die later by the bit of a horse.
Neptune unfurls a black sail for his men.
The fleet nears Gibraltar and Rocheval.

(CENTURY 1 – QUATRAIN 77)

This second quatrain describing the Battle of Trafalgar adds more detail. The promontory mentioned in the first line is Gibraltar, which stands between the Mediterranean and the Atlantic. The battle was fought between Gibraltar and Cape Roche – 'Rocheval'.

The commander of the French fleet, Admiral Villeneuve, was captured by the English but was returned to France the following year as part of a prisoner exchange scheme. Napoleon, enraged by his Admiral's incompetence at Trafalgar, had the unfortunate man assassinated by one of his Mamelukes. He was strangled at an Inn in Rennes and the weapon of choice was a horse's bridle – 'the bit of a horse'.

Admiral Lord Nelson was killed during the battle of Trafalgar, and on the voyage homeward his flagship, HMS Victory, unfurled black sails as a token of respect for the fallen commander.

MARRIAGE AND DIVORCE

Of a name never held by a Gallic King:
Never was so fearful a thunderbolt.
Italy, Spain and the English quake.
He will be greatly attentive to foreign women.

(CENTURY 4 – QUATRAIN 54)

This quatrain is one of only a handful in the *Centuries* that makes any references to Napoleon's private life. The last line predicts his fondness for foreign women. His first wife, Josephine, was a Creole; his second, Marie

Louise, was Austrian; and his mistress, Maria Walewska, was Polish.

The first line of this same quatrain refers to the fact that Napoleon introduced his own name to the French monarchy. Previously almost all French kings had been christened either Louis, Francis, Henri or Charles.

> **The divine curse will surprise the Great Prince**
> **Shortly after his marriage.**
> **Suddenly his allies and credit will vanish.**
> **The good sense of the man with cropped hair will die out.**

(CENTURY 1 – QUATRAIN 88)

When Napoleon divorced Josephine and married Marie Louise of Austria, he alienated many of his erstwhile supporters. Pope Pius VII, whose Papal States he wanted to control, excommunicated him, and there was a general public outcry against him. In spite of all his problems at home, however, Napoleon embarked upon his ill-fated Russian campaign.

THE PENINSULAR WARS

Those of Lerida will be in the Moselle,
Killing all those from the Loire and the Seine.
The seaside track will come near the high valley
When the Spanish open every route.

(CENTURY 1 – QUATRAIN 89)

In this quatrain, Nostradamus describes the period of the Peninsular Wars, when the British army, led by Wellington, were pushing up through Spain and Portugal, across the Pyrenees, and towards Bordeaux.

France will undertake a deadly voyage;
An army that has arrived by sea will march to the Pyrenees.
Spain will revolt; armies will march there,
And his ladies will be led back to France.

(CENTURY 4 – QUATRAIN 2)

This quatrain describes several different events in the Peninsular Wars. The Army which arrived by sea belonged to the British and was led by Wellington, and he did indeed march to the Pyrenees in 1808. Shortly before he arrived, the Spanish embarked upon their long and bloody war for independence from

France, and were therefore more than happy to allow Wellington, whom they now saw as a potential ally, to pass unhindered through their country.

FROM WELLINGTON'S PERSPECTIVE

Near the mountains of the Pyrenees,
A man will raise a great army against the Eagle.
Veins will open, and strength vanish:
The leader will pursue them as far as the Pau.

(CENTURY 4 – QUATRAIN 70)

Here Nostradamus describes Wellington's push through Spain and Portugal and into France via the Pyrenees. The 'Eagle' that confronts Wellington's 'great army' is, of course, Napoleon. The 'open veins' in the third line of the quatrains are thought to refer to the severing of French supply lines, which caused the French army to retreat to Pau.

DISASTER IN RUSSIA

A massed army approach from Slavonia.
The Destroyer will ruin the old city:
He will see his Roman Empire quite desolated,
Then would he not know how to extinguish the flame.

(CENTURY 4 – QUATRAIN 82)

There are several quatrains describing Napoleon's Russian campaign. The Emperor's march on Moscow was the greatest error in judgment in an otherwise brilliant military career. He miscalculated the level of resistance he would face, but worse than that, he failed to allow for the brutal Russian winter.

When the French army finally reached Moscow, the Russians had already abandoned the capital and, on the night of 14 September 1812, a handful of remaining Muscovites set fire to the city. Moscow, which was constructed almost entirely in wood, burned for three days and three nights. Napoleon and his Grand Army were powerless to stop the blaze and were forced to retreat to France.

THE RETREAT

The north wind will cause the siege to be halted,
To throw over the wall cinders, lime and dust;
Afterwards through rain which causes great hardship,
The last help is met at their frontier.

(CENTURY 9 – QUATRAIN 99)

This quatrain is generally considered to refer to the razing of Moscow and Napoleon's subsequent retreat. The `rain' which caused so much hardship was in fact snow. Hundreds of thousands of soldiers perished in the cold.

DESTRUCTION

The army, ready to fight, he will desert.
The chief adversary will be victorious.
The rear guard will make a defence.
Those who falter, die in the white country.

(CENTURY 4 – QUATRAIN 75)

Here Nostradamus describes the true scale of the Russian fiasco. The Emperor had led his Grand Army of half a million men into the country, and returned to France with a mere 20,000, most of them sick or wounded. During the long retreat through appalling conditions, many deserted. Some stood firm and fought a rear guard action against marauding Cossacks. As for Napoleon himself, he donned a disguise and rode back to France on a sledge, leaving his shattered army to fend for themselves. It is perhaps this act of supreme selfishness that Nostradamus is describing in the first line of the quatrain.

FROM ELBA TO WATERLOO

DEFEAT OF THE GRAND ARMY

**The Grand Army will be tracked down,
And at a certain moment will fail the King.
The promise given will be broken far away,
And he will find himself in pitiful disarray.**

(CENTURY 4 – QUATRAIN 22)

In this quatrain Nostradamus predicts the defeat of the new Grand Army. Despite his catastrophic campaign in Russia, Napoleon managed to raise a new army upon his return to France. He now faced attack from the Prussians, who had broken their alliance

with France – the promise 'broken far away' – as well as from
Britain, Russia and Sweden. Incredibly, he defeated the allies at
Lützen and Bautzen.

In 1814, France was invaded by the allies. Again Napoleon
defeated each army as it advanced on Paris, but ultimately he was
hopelessly outnumbered and, on 31 March, the allies took the capital.
Napoleon went into exile on to the Mediterranean island of Elba.

ELBA

The vanquished prince, prisoner in Italy,
Will cross the Gulf of Genoa towards Marseilles.
With great effort, the foreigners will conquer him.
Safe from shots, he will have powder instead of bees' honey.

(CENTURY 10 – QUATRAIN 24)

This is another prediction which contains an amazing amount of
detail. Early in 1815, news reached the exiled
Napoleon – 'the vanquished prince' – that he still
had the overwhelming support of the people of
France. In late February, he escaped from
his guards on the Island of Elba and sailed
with a handful of soldiers to France.
He landed at Cannes, near
Marseilles, on 1 March.
The Allies were
encamped near the
French frontiers, and

declared Napoleon 'outlawed from Europe'. Despite this, he managed to raise an army of more than 125,000 men and march north. He was, as Nostradamus predicted, destined to be conquered later that year at Waterloo.

THE HUNDRED DAYS

Despite great danger, the captive escapes.
In a short time his fortunes change dramatically.
The people are trapped in the palace,
By good fortune, the besieged city.

(CENTURY 2 – QUATRAIN 66)

In the first line of this quatrain, Nostradamus is referring to Napoleon's audacious escape from Elba on 1 March 1815. His fortunes did indeed change dramatically for the better in a very short time. Less than three weeks after he disembarked at Cannes, the exiled Emperor marched into Paris at the head of his new army. He made a triumphal procession through the streets of the capital. The Parisian mob took their lead from him and invaded the palace and court of the recently enthroned monarch, Louis XVIII. The King fled the city and Napoleon was carried shoulder high into the royal chambers. The crowd was so vast that no one could enter or leave the palace for several hours.

WATERLOO

**In the third month, at sunrise,
The Boar and the Leopard will meet on the battlefield.
The exhausted Leopard looks up to the heavens,
And sees an Eagle flying round the sun.**

(CENTURY 1 – QUATRAIN 23)

This is one of Nostradamus' most famous and intriguing quatrains, and one about which there is little argument. It is a description of the Battle of Waterloo, which was fought on 18 June 1815, just over three months after Napoleon's return to France.

To appreciate the quatrain fully, one must know the background to the battle. Blücher, the Prussian Boar, had been beaten back by Napoleon at Ligny, and this had prevented the Prussian troops from making their planned rendezvous with the British at Waterloo. The battle started at sunrise and the French troops battered the English Leopard (one of Nostradamus's descriptions of the English heraldic lion) until early evening, as Wellington awaited the arrival of his Prussian allies.

Wellington's position was facing south, and he would have seen Napoleon's Imperial Eagle standards silhouetted against the sun. The British army was exhausted and close to defeat when Wellington spotted a cloud of dust on the horizon. Blücher and his Prussian forces had arrived at last.

The Sun and the Eagle will appear to the victor.
The vanquished is reassured with a false promise.
Neither the bugle nor shouts will stop the fighters.
Liberty, if achieved in time, will be through death.

(CENTURY 1 – QUATRAIN 38)

This quatrain follows on directly from the one above, describing in detail the last hours of the Battle of Waterloo.

It was evening when Napoleon ordered the advance. He had spread a false rumour amongst his men that the approaching troops on their flank belonged to his ally Grouchy, rather than Blücher's Prussians.

Wellington must have seen the Imperial Eagles advancing in the evening sunshine. He knew that this would be a fight to the finish, and indeed it proved to be just that. When the French troops finally realised that the approaching troops were in fact Prussians, many of them broke rank and fled, and neither the shouts of their officers nor the buglers could bring them back into line. Napoleon's Grenadiers, however, fought valiantly to the last man.

Napoleon was captured and exiled to St Helena, and peace was restored to Europe by the political, if not actual death of the First Antichrist.

EXILE AND DEATH

The great Empire will soon be replaced by a small place
Which will soon begin to grow.
A small place of tiny area,
In the middle of which he will come to lay down his sceptre.

(CENTURY 1 – QUATRAIN 32)

After his defeat at Waterloo, Napoleon was exiled to the tiny, remote island of St. Helena in the South Atlantic. From there, there was no chance of a staging a second comeback. He spent the last few years of his life in miserable reflection on things that could have been.

ST. HELENA

The leader who led the people far from his own sky,
Will end his life in the middle of the sea on a rocky island,
With a population of 5,000, whose language and
customs are foreign.
The Leader will be kept in a barn in the middle of the sea.

(CENTURY 1 – QUATRAIN 98)

When Napoleon returned to Paris after his defeat at Waterloo, the Chamber demanded his abdication. He agreed to step down and asked to be taken to the United States of America, but the English Navy had blockaded the French coast and finally Napoleon elected to surrender himself to them. He thought he might receive better treatment at the hands of his erstwhile enemies than he would from his own people. He was wrong. The English treated him as a prisoner of war. They refused his request to go to America – they were afraid that he might stir up more trouble – and deported him to the tiny island of St Helena in the South Atlantic, almost 2,000 miles from the coast of Africa.

Napoleon's home for the last years of his life was Longwood House, which had originally been built as a barn for the island estate, and later converted into living quarters.

THE AFTERMATH

The inhuman tyrant shall die a hundred times,
And a wise man shall be put in his place.
He will have the whole senate in his hands,
But he will be troubled by a scoundrel.

(CENTURY 10 – QUATRAIN 90)

As Nostradamus predicted, every day on St Helena was a living death for the exiled Emperor. Back in Paris, the monarchy was restored in the person of King Louis XVIII. The parliament pledged allegiance to the new king to the last man.

CHAPTER 5

AFTER THE FALL

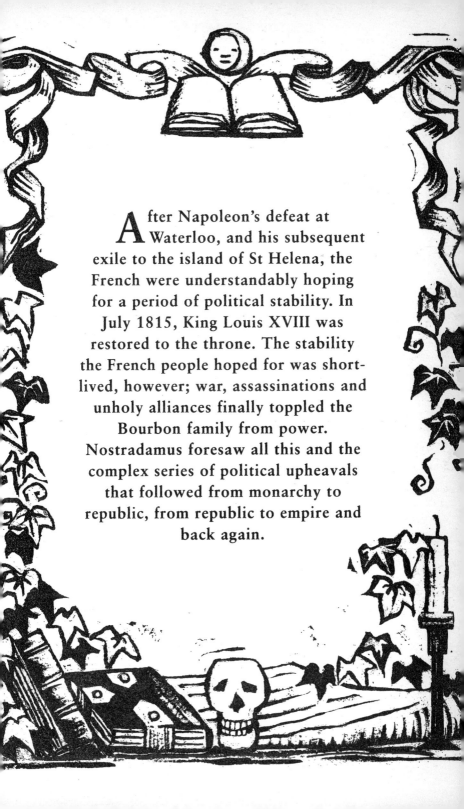

After Napoleon's defeat at Waterloo, and his subsequent exile to the island of St Helena, the French were understandably hoping for a period of political stability. In July 1815, King Louis XVIII was restored to the throne. The stability the French people hoped for was short-lived, however; war, assassinations and unholy alliances finally toppled the Bourbon family from power. Nostradamus foresaw all this and the complex series of political upheavals that followed from monarchy to republic, from republic to empire and back again.

RESTORATION OF THE MONARCHY

The blond man with the hooked nose will head the country,
Because of the mourning, and will drive out the others.
He will reinstate the exiles,
Sending the strongest beyond the seas.

(CENTURY 2 – QUATRAIN 67)

No sooner had the monarchy been restored than there was a revolt by nineteen army generals. They were arrested, tried and, together with thirty-eight other conspirators, permanently exiled from France. They were stripped of their civil rights and their lands and possessions were confiscated. Meanwhile, as Nostradamus predicted, less avowed Royalists were invited back from exile and their positions were restored.

ASSASSINATION OF THE DUKE DE BERRY

The moon, hidden by the clouds,
His brother becomes bright red.
The great one hidden for a great while in the shadows,
Will hold the blade in a bloody wound.

(CENTURY 1 – QUATRAIN 84)

The moon hidden by the clouds refers to the Count d'Artois, first cousin of the executed Louis XVI. He returned to France from many years in exile to become King Charles X. His son, the Duke de Berry, was assassinated at the Opera in Paris on 13 February, 1820. The duke's last words were, 'I am murdered. I am holding the hilt of the dagger.'

> **The leader from Fossano will have his throat cut,**
> **By the man who exercised the bloodhounds and the greyhounds.**
> **The deed will be committed by those of Tarpean rock**
> **When Saturn is in Leo on the thirteenth of February.**

(CENTURY 3 – QUATRAIN 96)

The 'leader from Fossano' in this quatrain is the Duke de Berry, whose maternal grandfather was King Fossano of Sardinia. His killer, a man called Louvel, worked in the royal stables, where hounds as well as horses were kept. The Tarpean rock is the cliff from which criminals were thrown as a form of execution in Republican Rome.

The astrological reference in the last line of the quatrain accurately pinpoints the date of the Duke's assassination.

The nephew shall demonstrate great courage.
The crime committed by a cowardly heart.
The Duke will try Ferrara and Asti;
When the comedy takes place in the evening.

(CENTURY 4 – QUATRAIN 73)

As predicted by this third quatrain about the assassination, the Duke de Berry was indeed stabbed when leaving a comic opera. The nephew mentioned in the first line is none other than Napoleon III, who was destined to become ruler of France as a direct result of the murder.

THE LAST OF THE CONDES

The last of the line will be strangled in his bed,
Because of his involvement with a blond woman.
The Empire, exhausted, will be replaced by the Third.
He will be put to death because of his will, with linen.

(CENTURY 1 – QUATRAIN 39)

Louis-Henri-Joseph, Duke of Bourbon, Prince of Condé, was found hanged in his bedroom on August 10, 1830. The murder weapon was two linen handkerchiefs. The Condé dynasty died with him.

The blond woman implicated in the second line of the quatrain was Sophie Dawes, his mistress, who was married to one of the Duke's household, the Baron de Feucheres. A manipulative woman, Sophie persuaded her lover to change his will favouring the Duke of Bordeaux and herself. The 'Third' is generally considered to refer to the Third Republic.

THE ACCESSION OF LOUIS PHILIPPE

**The great one will no longer dream,
Unease will replace repose.
The phalanx of gold, blue and vermilion,
Will subdue Africa and gnaw it to the bone.**

(CENTURY 5 – QUATRAIN 69)

In 1830, Charles X abdicated after a revolution. His uncle, Louis Philippe, Duke d'Orléans, took the throne. He was the first Bourbon to adopt the tricolore as the French national flag. Nostradamus was slightly off the mark with gold, but he did get the other two colours right. The reign of Louis Philippe saw the French conquering and colonising North Africa.

CONQUEST AND REBELLION

Fortune will smile on Philippe for seven years.
He will conquer the barbarian.
Then there will be trouble with a contrary affair,
And young Ogmios will usurp his stronghold.

(CENTURY 9 – QUATRAIN 89)

As Nostradamus predicted, the first seven years of Louis Philippe's reign were extremely successful. He defeated the Arab armies in North Africa and occupied Algeria.

In 1842, however, tragedy befell the King. His son and heir, Ferdinand-Philippe-Louis-Charles-Henri-Rose of Orléans, was killed in an accident. At the same time, there was considerable civil unrest – Louis Philippe's illiberal home policies were much less popular than his foreign ones – and rebel forces attacked the royal palace. In 1848, the king abdicated in favour of his grandson, but a provisional government was accepted by popular acclaim and a democratic Republic succeeded the monarchy.

DEATH OF THE HEIR

The King's eldest son, on a runaway horse,
Will fall head-first at a gallop, the horse's mouth being
injured.
With the rider's foot caught, groaning, dragged and pulled,
He will die horribly.

(CENTURY 7 – QUATRAIN 38)

Louis Philippe's eldest son was due to inspect French troops at St. Omer in July 1842. He took a carriage to Neuilly to say goodbye to his parents before leaving. En route, his horses bolted. The young prince was flung from the carriage and smashed his skull on the road.

NAPOLEON III & THE THIRD REPUBLIC

ACCESSION

Originating from a weak country and poor birth,
At the end of its tether and wanting peace,
he will succeed to the Empire.
He will then rule the young republic.
Such a disastrous person never achieved power.

(CENTURY 3 – QUATRAIN 28)

In 1848, after the abdication of Louis Philippe, the Third Republic
was established and Louis Napoleon, nephew of Napoleon Bonaparte,
was elected president. In 1851, he dissolved the Assembly and
assumed new powers, making himself president for ten years. The
following year, he proclaimed France an Empire, with himself at its
head as Napoleon III (Napoleon II, the only son of Napoleon
Bonaparte, had died in 1832).

His reign lasted less than twenty years and was
fairly disastrous. For the first time in 400 years,
France's territory actually shrank with the loss of
Alsace-Lorraine.

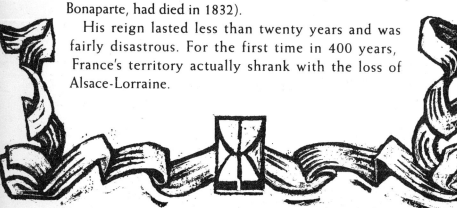

ANNEXATION OF ALSACE-LORRAINE

Some of the lowest parts of the country of Lorraine
Will be united with lower Germany.
Through the people of the seats of Picardy,
Normandy and Maine,
They will be reunited to the cantons.

(CENTURY 10 – QUATRAIN 51)

As Nostradamus predicted, Lorraine and Alsace were ceded to
lower Germany by the French – the people of Picardy, Normandy
and Maine – after the disastrous Franco-Prussian War, which
ended with the fall of Paris in 1871. The lands were not returned
to France until 1919.

THE ORSINI AFFAIR

A French leader, wounded in conflict,
Seeing death overcome his people near the theatre,
Hard pressed by his enemies amid blood and wounded,
Will be helped by the crowd and four.

(CENTURY 5 – QUATRAIN 10)

On 14 January 1858, Napoleon III and the Empress Eugénie were due to attend the opera. Their landau was passing along the Rue le Pelletier when there were three loud explosions. The bombs, which were presumably meant for the Emperor, killed ten civilians and wounded more than 150 others. Napoleon and Eugénie escaped serious injury.

Felice Orsini, an Italian nationalist revolutionary, was accused of masterminding the assassination attempt. He was tried, condemned to death and guillotined on 13 March 1858.

THE FALL OF NAPOLEON III

**Instead of the great man, who will be rejected out of prison,
His friend will take power in his place.
Monarchical power will be shackled within six months,
stillborn;
The monarchy will be abandoned by vote, after the rivers
freeze over.**

(CENTURY 6 – QUATRAIN 52)

Napoleon III's surrender at Sedan in 1870 spelt the end of the Second Empire. Paris was under siege by the Germans throughout one of the coldest winters in living memory.

Patrice de MacMahon, a general and friend of Napoleon III, was captured at Sedan. He spent some time as a prisoner of war, then, after the Paris treaty, took command of the Versailles army and suppressed the Commune, the revolutionary government that had formed in Paris. In 1873, he was elected President of the new Republic for a term of seven years, but was accused of reactionary and monarchical leanings and was forced to resign in 1879.

DEATH OF NAPOLEON III

**When the deserter of the great fortress
Has abandoned the place,
The enemy will perform feats of prowess,
And the Emperor will die soon afterwards.**

(CENTURY 4 – QUATRAIN 65)

On 14 August 1870, when Napoleon III and his armies were forced to retreat from Metz, he was assured by Marshal François Bazaine that his forces would rendezvous with those of the Emperor at Sedan. This was a deliberate lie. The Marshal's treachery led directly to Napoleon's undoing.

Like his forebear, Napoleon III went into exile, but not as far as St Helena. He joined his wife at Chislehurst in Kent, where he died in 1873, at the age of sixty-five.

GARIBALDI & ITALY'S WAR OF LIBERATION

Nostradamus wrote several quatrains about Italy's fight to liberate herself from the grip of Austria. More specifically, the prophet seemed interested in Giuseppe Garibaldi, the patriot and revolutionary who helped Victor Emmanuel II unite North and South to create modern Italy.

> **With more than ten coming from Langeudoc and Guyenne,**
> **The thousand wished to return to Italy.**
> **The Duke of Savoy will march against the people of**
> **Southern Italy.**
> **They will succeed in recovering Savoy and Naples.**

(CENTURY 7 – QUATRAIN 31)

In 1859, Victor Emmanuel II, king of Sardinia, was supported by France in his war against Austria. As part of the deal, he annexed Lombardy, Tuscany, Parma, Moderna and Romagna, while ceding Nice and Savoy to France.

In May 1860, Garibaldi – who, ironically, had been born in Nice – joined the fray. He sailed from Genoa with a small volunteer army and landed in Sicily. He assisted the Mazzinian rebels in their fight to liberate the island from Napoleon's rule. Crossing with his army to the mainland, he swiftly overran much of southern Italy, and drove the King of Naples from his capital.

GARIBALDI'S THOUSAND

The city whose freedom has been reduced by slavery,
Having become free will give asylum to the dreamers.
Having boldly changed the king,
They will go from a hundred to more than a thousand.

(CENTURY 4 – QUATRAIN 16)

The city in question in the first line of this quatrain is Genoa, where Garibaldi established his headquarters. On 5 May 1860, Garibaldi stood on Piedmont (Genoa) bridge and asked 'How many of us are there?' 'More than a thousand,' came the reply, 'including sailors.' In fact his 'thousand' were 1049 strong.

This tiny army sailed to Sicily and captured the telegraph office at Marsala, whence Garibaldi transmitted false messages to confuse the enemy. He soon conquered the Island, then under the control of the King of Naples, and crossed to the mainland. He went on to capture Naples and proclaim himself dictator of the Two Sicilies in the name of Victor Emmanuel, King of Italy.

RISE AND FALL OF GARIBALDI

**The powerful soldier from Nice
Will not be defeated in battle, but by money.
His deeds will be the cause of debate for many years.
This foreigner will strike terror in the hearts of the
bourgeoisie.**

(CENTURY 7 – QUATRAIN 19)

The 'powerful soldier from Nice' was Giuseppe Garibaldi, who was born there in 1802. From an early age he was an idealist, dreaming of adventure, freedom, and social justice for all. He pursued his dreams by leading guerrilla campaigns in both Europe and South America, and became a folk hero. He was, however, bitterly opposed by the conservative bourgeoisie, who considered him a subversive revolutionary.

As Nostradamus predicted, Garibaldi was not defeated in battle, but by money. In 1873, his fighting days over, he retired to Caprera and set about writing his memoirs. He was not a literary success and, crippled by arthritis and unable to work, he was forced to sell his only real asset, his yacht. He received 80,000 lira for the vessel, a fraction of its true worth, and entrusted the money to his ex-comrade in arms, Antonio Bo, who in turn promised to bank it for him in Genoa. Instead of banking the money, however, Bo absconded to America and was never heard of again. Penniless and crippled by his many wounds, Garibaldi lived in relative obscurity until his death in 1882.

INVENTIONS AND TECHNICAL DEVELOPMENTS

The latter part of the nineteenth century was a time of extraordinary technical innovation. It is hardly surprising, therefore, that Nostradamus foresaw some of these developments. Typically, many of the inventions that captured his imagination were instruments of war and destruction, in keeping with his propensity for the apocalyptic.

MONTGOLFIER'S BALLOON

**There will depart from Mont Gaulfier and Aventine,
One who through a hole will warn the army.
The booty will be taken from between two rocks,
The renown of Sextus, the celibate will fail.**

(CENTURY 5 – QUATRAIN 57)

In 1773, the hot air balloon was invented by the Montgolfier brothers. It was used for scouting by the French army at the Battle of Fleurus in 1794. The French victory at Fleurus was a turning point in the Revolutionary Wars, paving the way for the sack of Rome.

The last lines of the quatrain are totally unconnected with the balloon and refer to the harrowing of the clergy by Napoleon.

LOUIS PASTEUR

The lost thing is discovered after many centuries.
Pasteur will be celebrated almost as a god-like figure.
This is when the moon completes her great cycle,
But by other rumours he shall be dishonoured.

(CENTURY 1 – QUATRAIN 25)

This is one of Nostradamus' most impressive quatrains, not only because it actually mentions Pasteur by name, but also because it puts a date on the establishment of his Institute.

Louis Pasteur's discovery that airborne micro-organisms spread disease was one of the most exciting breakthroughs in modern medicine. He founded the Pasteur Institute on 14 November 1889. The cycle of the moon ran from 1535 to 1889.

The dishonour mentioned in the last line of the quatrain refers to the hostile reception with which his discoveries were received by members of the French Academy. For years he was labelled as a fraud and a quack.

SUBMARINES

Through lightning in a box, gold and silver will be melted,
The two captives will devour one another.
The greatest of the city stretched,
When the fleet travels under water.

(CENTURY 3 – QUATRAIN 13)

This is a complex quatrain which seems to cover a number of different technical developments. The first line would appear to predict new alloys created under intense temperature or possibly a new source of power.

The last line quite clearly predicts the invention of the submarine and the use of the word 'fleet' suggests that Nostradamus thought the invention would be used in warfare.

MISSILES AND ROCKETS

The brave eldest son of a King's daughter,
Will drive the Celts back very far.
He will use thunderbolts, so many and in such an array,
Few and distant, then deep into the West.

(CENTURY 4 – QUATRAIN 99)

The Celts referred to in this quatrain are probably the Bretons. Nostradamus suggests that they will be driven back after being confronted by some frightful new type of weapon which could be launched at extremely long range. This suggests either mortar shells, missiles or rockets carrying explosive warheads.

AIR TRAVEL

Pestilences extinguished, the world will become smaller.
For a long time, the world will live in peace.
People will travel safely through the sky, over land and sea,
Then war will break out again.

(CENTURY 1 – QUATRAIN 63)

'Pestilence extinguished' probably refers to the period between 1900 and 1914, when the western world was comparatively free from war and natural disasters. It was during this time, in 1903, that Orville and Wilbur Wright launched their heavier-than-air flying machine, making the world 'smaller'. By the outbreak of World War I, mentioned in the last line of the quatrain, aircraft were well established both as a means of travel and as an instrument of war.

CHAPTER 6

FROM THE GREAT WAR TO THE RUSSIAN REVOLUTION

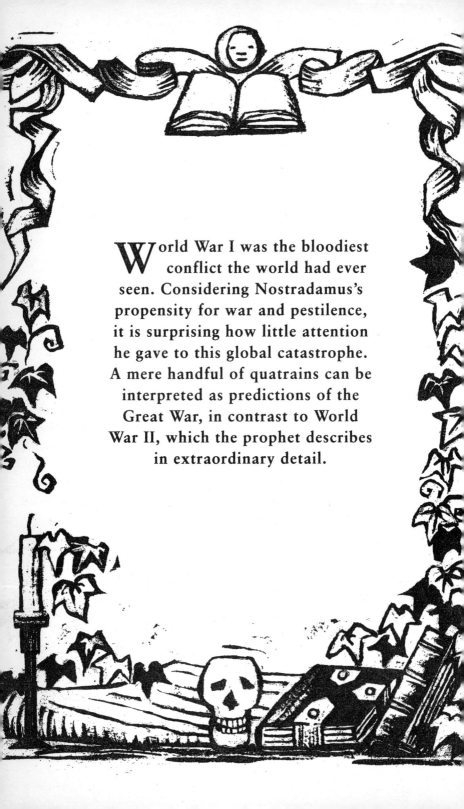

World War I was the bloodiest conflict the world had ever seen. Considering Nostradamus's propensity for war and pestilence, it is surprising how little attention he gave to this global catastrophe. A mere handful of quatrains can be interpreted as predictions of the Great War, in contrast to World War II, which the prophet describes in extraordinary detail.

THE GREAT WAR

**After a considerable period of easy living,
Several areas around Rheims will be smitten from the sky.
Oh what a bloody conflict is nearing them;
Fathers, sons and governors will not dare approach
these places.**

(CENTURY 3 – QUATRAIN 18)

This one quatrain covers the entire span of the Great War.

The early years of the twentieth century, as Nostradamus predicted, were relatively trouble free in Europe. By 1913, though, conflict on the continent looked inevitable. Germany had poured formidable sums of money into war materials, and France had responded by passing a law which increased national service from two years to three.

On 27 May 1918, as the war approached its conclusion, the Germans launched a surprise offensive and shattered the French front between Soissons and Rheims. Convinced that he could defeat the French totally, General Erich von Ludendorff launched a second attack on General Foch's troops along a fifty-mile front on either side of the Rheims Salient. Ludendorff, however, had badly underestimated the skill and courage of his adversary, and the ensuing battle of the Marne proved to be turning point in the war in favour of the Allies.

France may have achieved victory, but it was at a terrible price. In four years of fighting she had more casualties than any other country, with one and a half million dead and three million wounded. Many of her great cities – Rheims, Arras, Soissons, Verdun and St Quentin – had been reduced to rubble.

Another interesting feature of this particular quatrain is to be found in the second line – 'Rheims will be smitten from the sky'. Nostradamus might be referring either to aerial bombardment or to shelling by heavy artillery, neither of which existed in the prophet's own time.

THE DARDANELLES

**Towards Aquitaine, by British assaults,
And then by them also great incursions.
Rains and forest make the terrain unsafe.
Against Port Selin they will make mighty invasions.**

(CENTURY 2 – QUATRAIN 1)

This is one of Nostradamus's most lucid quatrains dealing with World War I. In 1915, when France – 'Aquitaine' – and Britain were bogged down on the Western Front, Churchill instigated a second front against Turkey. The allied forces launched their attack on the Dardanelles, hoping to take Constantinople – 'Port Selin'. The campaign was ultimately a failure, doomed in part by the appalling weather conditions mentioned in the third line of the quatrain.

BARTER IN THE FIELD

The whole army will be exhausted by the long war,
So no money will be found for the troops.
Instead of gold or silver, leather will be minted.
The brass of France and the crescent of the moon.

(CENTURY 7 – QUATRAIN 25)

The middle two lines of this quatrain are particularly interesting. It is widely thought that Nostradamus was predicting the demise of gold and silver currency. He could not conceive that anyone would accept anything as flimsy as paper for a cash payment and therefore he assumed it would be 'minted in leather'.

The last line of the quatrain is open to several interpretations. J H Brennan puts forward the idea that the word 'brass' means war, as in the biblical 'Sounding brass' and that the 'crescent moon' represents the flag of Turkey, against whom the French fought.

A simpler interpretation, however, would be that the line refers again to currency, now minted in alloys of base metals and silver – the moon being a common metaphor for the latter.

GERMANY'S DEFEAT

The greatest army will be put to flight,
But they will not be pursued beyond the river.
The troops will bivouac, the army much reduced.
It will be chased out of France.

(CENTURY 4 – QUATRAIN 12)

Despite having mobilised more than fourteen million men during the Great War, the Germans were faced with defeat in 1918. The November Armistice conditions demanded that all German troops be evacuated from France, Belgium and Alsace-Lorraine within two weeks. They were also obliged to evacuate the left bank of the Rhine, which would then be occupied by the Allies. The most important condition from the French point of view was the return of Alsace-Lorraine, which she had lost as a result of the Franco-Prussian War.

THE GREAT FLU EPIDEMIC

The dreadful war which began in the west;
The year after will come pestilence
So dreadful for the young, old and the beasts.
Blood, fire, Mercury, Mars, Jupiter and France.

(CENTURY 9 – QUATRAIN 55)

No sooner was the Great War over than the 'pestilence' predicted by Nostradamus struck. It came in the form of an epidemic of a particularly virulent form of viral influenza which swept through mainland Europe and Great Britain. The disease killed more people in a single winter than had died in the entire four years of military conflict.

THE FALL OF THE HAPSBURGS

When the great trees tremble in the south wind,
Covered with blood,
So great an assembly will pour forth from Vienna,
And the land of Austria will quake.

(CENTURY 1 – QUATRAIN 82)

In November 1918, during a violent storm, the ancient Hapsburg dynasty, rulers of Austria for more than 600 years, was overthrown after huge demonstrations by students and workers in Vienna. Austria became a democratic republic.

THE RUSSIAN REVOLUTION

The Great War was without question the most momentous event in western Europe during the early twentieth century, but something of even greater political significance was brewing to the east. The rise of the Bolsheviks and the Russian Revolution did not escape the prophet's attention, nor did the fate of the Romanov dynasty.

THE TSARINA AND RASPUTIN

With the pretence of divine fury,
Will the wife of the great leader be violated.
Judges wishing to damn such a situation,
Sacrifice their victim with ignorant prejudice.

(CENTURY 6 – QUATRAIN 72)

The 'wife of the great leader' who is 'violated' in the second line of this quatrain is Alexandra Fyodorovna, Empress of Russia and consort to the last Tsar, Nicholas II. She was a powerful and determined woman who systematically usurped her husband's authority to the point where she became virtual ruler of Russia. The Tsarina's downfall came because of her association with the self-proclaimed holy man, faith healer and libertine, Grigoriy Rasputin. Rasputin demonstrated his powers to the Tsarina by healing her haemophiliac son, the Tsarevich Alexei in 1905, saving his life on several occasions. From that time on, Rasputin, a Siberian peasant by birth, lived at the royal palace and exerted enormous power over the entire Romanov family. Rasputin, despite being nominally a monk, was a notorious womaniser and drunk. Soon rumours were flying around that the Tsarina herself could be numbered amongst his sexual conquests.

In the Great War, with Nicholas absent at the front, Rasputin virtually ruled Russia, and in 1916 a group of aristocrats, appalled by the situation, conspired to kill him. First they poisoned his wine with cyanide and then, when this had no effect on him, they shot him five times and bludgeoned him over the head. Still Rasputin refused to die. He was eventually thrown, bound and chained, into the River Neva, where he drowned.

THE OCTOBER REVOLUTION

Here is the month, infamous for the ills it will bring.
All those following the red flag will bring death, famine
and civil war.
Opponents will be exiled and it will be impossible to
prevent the leader's death,
Which will long remain a secret.

(PRESAGE 89 – OCTOBER)

The Tsar abdicated in February 1917, and Russia became a Republic. By October 1917, the political and economic situation in the country was catastrophic. There was widespread civil unrest. Workers, 'red guards', and disenchanted soldiers and sailors stormed the Winter Palace, and placed members of the government under arrest. At Petrograd and Moscow, the army attempted to quash the revolution and restore the government. They failed and, on 1 November 1917, the Bolsheviks triumphed.

Members of the former royal family were arrested and disappeared. Rumours abounded that they had been exiled or put to death. Only very recently has proof emerged that they were in fact executed en masse at Ekaterinburg.

MASSACRE OF THE ROMANOVS

The blood of the innocents, widow and virgin,
So many evils will be committed by means of the Great
Red One.
Holy images placed over burning candles.
Terrified, none will be seen to move.

(CENTURY 8 – QUATRAIN 80)

According to long-suppressed Bolshevik accounts, shortly after midnight on 17 July 1918, Tsar Nicholas and eleven members of the Romanov family and their entourage were taken to the basement of the Ipatyev house in Ekaterinburg. Minutes later, an execution squad arrived. As the family huddled in a corner, they opened fire. The shooting lasted for more than twenty minutes. Tsarevich Alexei and three of his sisters were wounded but still alive. The executioners finished off the survivors with knives. Afterwards, the bodies were dismembered and thrown into a pit of acid.

The last line of the quatrain suggests that none of the Romanovs survived and that the claims of Anna Anderson, who maintained for decades that she was the Tsar's daughter, Anastasia, are fraudulent.

THE SPREAD OF COMMUNISM

**The songs and demands of the Russians,
Whose heads of state imprison their own people,
Will be accepted by holy writ,
Only by the feeble minded.**

(CENTURY 1 – QUATRAIN 14)

As Nostradamus predicts in this quatrain, the new Russian government criminalised their political opposition. Purges were directed at counter-revolutionaries. To accommodate them all, new jails were built. Three of the five prisons in Moscow were reserved exclusively for political prisoners. Forced labour camps were also established in Siberia and other remote regions of the newly formed Soviet Union, and these housed hundreds of thousands of dissenters at any one time.

Russia will derive such power through the war,
That she will change her prince for a provincial by birth,
Then his power will win the sea,
And will raise troops beyond the mountains.

(CENTURY 5 – QUATRAIN 26)

Bolshevik Russia, under the charge of the provincial politician, Lenin, retired from the war in March 1918. The Allies initially supported the new Russian regime, but this support soon evaporated, when it became clear that Russia had ambitions to spread Communism beyond its boundaries.

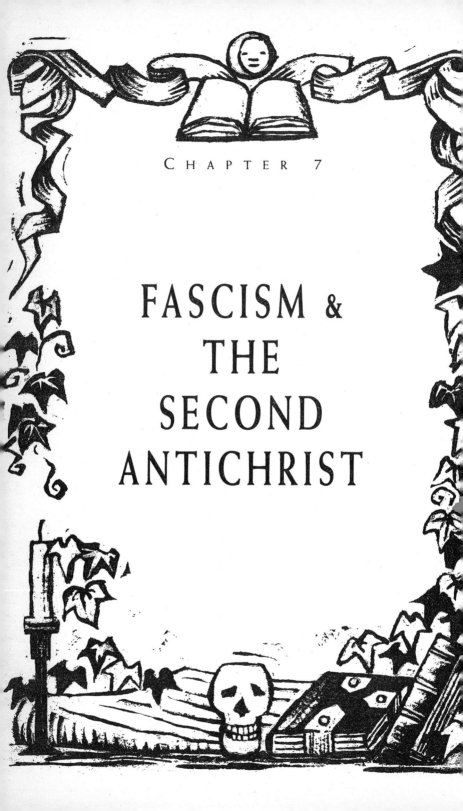

CHAPTER 7

FASCISM & THE SECOND ANTICHRIST

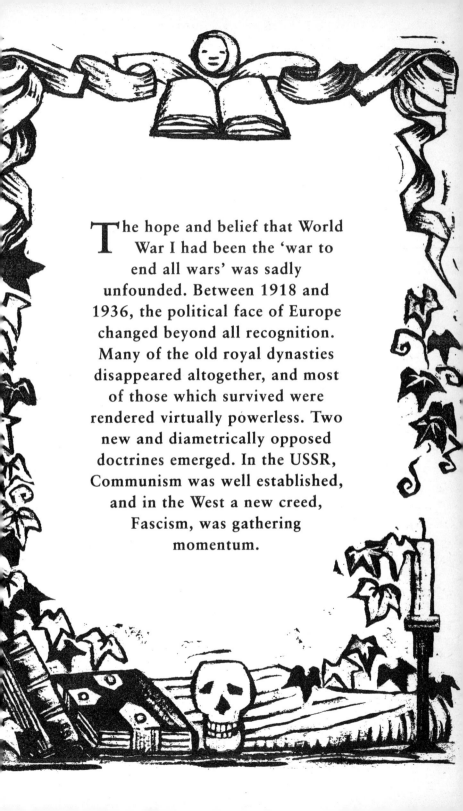

The hope and belief that World War I had been the 'war to end all wars' was sadly unfounded. Between 1918 and 1936, the political face of Europe changed beyond all recognition. Many of the old royal dynasties disappeared altogether, and most of those which survived were rendered virtually powerless. Two new and diametrically opposed doctrines emerged. In the USSR, Communism was well established, and in the West a new creed, Fascism, was gathering momentum.

Fascism first manifested itself in Italy as a direct response to the spread of communism. The word fascist derives from the Latin *fasces*, an ancient Roman symbol of authority consisting of a bundle of rods and an axe. The author of the party's manifesto was a revolutionary nationalist and newspaper editor, Benito Mussolini, known as Il Duce.

Mussolini's political stance was soon emulated in other parts of Europe, notably Spain and Germany. The movement produced three of the great anti-heroes of the twentieth century, Mussolini himself, Francisco Franco, and Adolf Hitler, Nostradamus's second antichrist. The prophet predicted the rise to power of all three.

BENITO MUSSOLINI

A great man will be born in Verona and Vincenza,
Who carries a very unworthy surname.
He who at Venice will desire vengeance,
Himself taken by a man of watch and sign.

(CENTURY 8 – QUATRAIN 33)

The 'great man' is Mussolini, who was born in northern Italy, not far from Verona, in 1883. His name literally translated means muslin-maker, an undistinguished title for what was considered an undistinguished trade. He was in fact born into the working class. His father, a blacksmith and a socialist, was the antithesis of the established ruling order.

IL DUCE'S RISE TO POWER

The first great prize will be the prince of Pescheria,
Then will come a cruel and wicked man.
In Venice he will lose his arrogant ways,
And will be led into evil by young Selin.

(CENTURY 8 – QUATRAIN 31)

In 1919, Mussolini and a group of war veterans founded the Fasci di Combattimento, a revolutionary nationalist group. The movement soon gained considerable support from Italian landowners, industrialists and ex-army officers. In the early days, Mussolini's blackshirts fought at a local level against communists, catholics, socialists and liberals, all opponents of the fascist doctrine.

Mussolini's first real success came on October 28 1922, when he secured a mandate from King Victor Emmanuel III, Prince of Pescheria, to form a coalition government. Three years later, he dissolved this government and imposed a one-party, totalitarian dictatorship with himself at the head. From this time on he was to be known as Il Duce. In later quatrains, Nostradamus actually refers to Mussolini by this adopted title.

Il Duce & Victor Emmanuel

The King will discover that which he covets so greatly,
When the Prelate is wrongly taken.
His reply to the Duce will enrage him,
Who, in Milan, will put several to death.

(CENTURY 6 – QUATRAIN 31)

King Victor Emmanuel loathed Mussolini's strutting arrogance and took enormous pleasure in making him angry. The 'Prelate' mentioned in the second line of the quatrain was most probably Pope Pius XII, who incurred severe criticism after World War II for turning a blind eye to German extermination camps and other Nazi atrocities. Those put to death, in the last line, must certainly have included Count Ciano, the Italian Foreign Minister and Mussolini's son-in-law. He was executed after he was discovered conspiring with others to over throw Il Duce in 1943.

THE DEATH OF MUSSOLINI

**A new faction will lead the army,
Cut off to the river bank,
Waiting for help from the Milanese elite;
Il Duce loses his eyes in an iron cage.**

(CENTURY 9 – QUATRAIN 95)

This is the second reference to Mussolini by his adopted name, Il Duce, in a Nostradamus quatrain. The prophet was slightly off target when describing the manner of the dictator's death – 'Il Duce loses his eyes in an iron cage' – but there are some remarkable similarities to his real end. His death was violent, and his body was put on public display in Milan. In reality, the dictator was shot, his body first hanged from a lamp post, then shown to the public hanging upside down from a meat hook.

FRANCO AND THE SPANISH CIVIL WAR

The second of the great fascist leaders who attracted the attention of Nostradamus was Francisco Franco, who led the Nationalist forces to victory in the Spanish Civil War, which broke out in 1936. He ruled Spain as a virtual dictator until his death in 1975, at which point the Monarchy was restored. In a handful of quatrains, the prophet not only mentions Franco by name, but also tracks his life and career with astonishing accuracy.

FRANCO'S RISE TO POWER

From Castille, Franco will drive out the Assembly.
The Ambassador will not agree, and a schism will occur.
Followers of Rivera will be in the throng,
And entry to the great gulf will be prevented.

(CENTURY 9 – QUATRAIN 16)

This is without question one of the most impressive of quatrains. It mentions not only Franco himself, but also Primo de Rivera, dictator of Spain since 1923, and Franco's arch enemy.

When Franco invaded Spain from his base in Morocco, he

was intent on bringing down the National Assembly, headed by de Rivera. There followed the greatest 'schism' Spain had ever known, the Spanish Civil War. The war was expected to be over in matter of months, even weeks, but in fact it raged on for almost three years, with a terrible loss of life. When the war finally ended in 1939, Franco added to the death toll by ordering the execution of hundreds of thousands of Loyalist supporters.

The last line of the quatrain is out of sequence. The 'great gulf' refers to the Mediterranean. In 1936, Franco had been exiled to the Canary Islands and forbidden to return to his native Spain.

THE CIVIL WAR

A great man will flee to Spain,
Which will bleed from a great wound.
Troops will pass over high mountains.
All will be laid waste, then he will rule in peace.

(CENTURY 3 – QUATRAIN 54)

In 1936, Franco left the Canary Islands, where he was exiled, and travelled to Morocco. From there he crossed the Mediterranean to Spain and started the revolution which became the Spanish Civil War.

The 'great wound' mentioned in the second line of the quatrain was the terrible loss of life suffered by Spaniards on both sides of the conflict. In three years of fighting, in excess of 600,000 men died, and countless numbers more were injured.

The troops who passed over 'high mountains' were 50,000 German and 10,000 Italian reinforcements who fought for Franco, and 20,000 Russians who sided with the Loyalist army. All these men entered Spain by crossing the Pyrenees.

In the last line of the quatrain, Nostradamus foresees a peaceful future for Spain after the war. This turned out to be true. Despite the repressive nature of Franco's dictatorship, Spain remained neutral during World War II, and has not been involved in any major conflict since that time.

FASCIST ALLIES

From the furthest part of Spain,
Will come an officer who will travel the confines of Europe.
At the moment the revolution arrives by the sea of Llanes,
The revolutionaries will be defeated by his great army.

(CENTURY 10 – QUATRAIN 48)

This is another quatrain which gives a very general picture of the Spanish Civil War. The second line suggests Franco's request for help from other European powers, help which was forthcoming from Italy and Germany, both of which had adopted fascist regimes.

MASSACRE OF THE INNOCENTS

**A flame will engulf the Republic,
Which will want to put Innocents to death.
The forces will be inflamed,
When they have seen monstrous things in Seville.**

(CENTURY 6 – QUATRAIN 19)

As Nostradamus rightly predicted in this quatrain, Franco took terrible retribution upon those who had opposed him during the Civil War. Countless Loyalists, including members of the clergy, were summarily executed. One of the main venues for these atrocities was Seville. It is hardly surprising that there was outrage amongst ordinary Spaniards.

ADOLF HITLER – THE SECOND ANTICHRIST

After the horrors and bloodshed of the Civil War, Spain was destined to enjoy half a century of relative stability. This was not true of the rest of the world, which was about to be plunged into the most comprehensive war mankind had ever experienced. Its roots lay in a particularly vicious offshoot of fascism, Nazism, an ideology developed and nurtured by the National Socialist German Workers Party.

The terms of the Treaty of Versailles, which formally ended World War I, left Germany economically and socially crippled. Sandwiched between its ex-enemies and an ambitiously expansionist communist state, it was a ripe breeding ground for extreme, ultra-nationalistic political movements. The National Socialist German Workers Party, formed in Munich in 1921, was one of the more extreme parties that blossomed during this period. The German authorities thought that the National Socialists might be a cover for communist insurgents and sent a young ex-army corporal to infiltrate the movement and report back his findings. The corporal was Adolf Hitler, Nostradamus's second Antichrist.

Hitler attended several National Socialist meetings and discovered that, far from being a communist cell, the party had a philosophy that was ultra right wing and nationalistic, a philosophy with which he could readily identify. So, rather than spying on the party, Hitler joined it with the clear ambition of becoming its leader. Within a year he had achieved his aim.

From its humble beginnings in the beer cellars of Munich, the party grew rapidly under Hitler's leadership. In 1923, together with several other extreme right wing parties, he attempted to overthrow the Bavarian government, but the putsch failed and Hitler was imprisoned for nine months. It was during this period of incarceration that he dictated his infamous work, *Mein Kampf*, to his friend and colleague, Rudolph Hess. The book formed the basis of Nazi policy, which defined the enemies of Germany as the Jews, communism, effete liberalism, and decadent capitalism. It was a blueprint for a regime which Hitler himself was destined to lead, and, by the late 1930s, it was required reading in Germany, outselling the *Holy Bible* three to one.

On his release from prison, Hitler gathered around him a clique of devoted followers who would later form his government. They included Josef Goebbels, Heinrich Himmler and Hermann Goering. In 1932, Hitler stood for the German presidency and lost by a narrow margin. The Nazi party, though, held the greatest number of seats in the Reichstag. The following year, Nazi supremacy was so apparent that Hindenbürg, the President of the Republic, had no option but to name Hitler Chancellor of Germany.

Once in power, Hitler suspended free elections and banned all other political parties. Even his own party members were not safe. In the infamous 'Night of the Long Knives', he had his elite bodyguard hunt down and murder about a hundred party members whom he considered dissident. Hindenbürg died in August 1934, and Hitler immediately assumed the role of president and assumed the title of Führer, supreme leader, of the Third Reich.

Nostradamus wrote scores of quatrains which have been interpreted as references to Hitler's life and career. In some of them he actually refers to the Führer by name. He describes him as Hi$ter which is not only remarkably close to his name, but is also the Latin word for the River Danube, near whose shores Hitler was raised in Linz, Austria.

THE BIRTH AND DEATH OF
THE SECOND ANTI-CHRIST

**Near the Rhine, from the Noric Alps,
A great leader of people will be born too late.
He will defend himself against Russia and Hungary;
What becomes of him will never be known.**

(CENTURY 3 – QUATRAIN 58)

This quatrain spans Hitler's whole life. He was born on 20 April 1889, at Braunau-am-Inn in Austria, the son of a minor customs official. The reference to him being 'born too late' reflects the fact that the type of Empire he envisaged building was, by the twentieth century, an outdated concept.

The prophet saves the most interesting line of the quatrain for last. It is widely assumed that Hitler committed suicide alongside his mistress, Eva Braun, in his bunker in Berlin as the city was being overrun by the Russians. The bodies found in the bunker, however, were burned with petrol and could never be satisfactorily identified. Since that time, stories have been rife about the Führer's escape to South America. Most authorities consider this extremely unlikely, but the fact remains that Hitler is probably the only great world leader whose end is open to question.

ORIGINS

From the depths of Western Europe,
To poor people a child will be born.
With his tongue, he will seduce a great mass of people.
His reputation will grow even greater in an eastern Empire.

(CENTURY 3 – QUATRAIN 35)

This is the first of several quatrains which has been interpreted as referring to either Hitler or Napoleon. Both were born of humble parents in politically remote parts of Europe, and both were famous for their powers of oratory. It is the last line of the verse which makes one come down in favour of Hitler. The 'eastern Empire' clearly refers to Japan, which eventually became his ally.

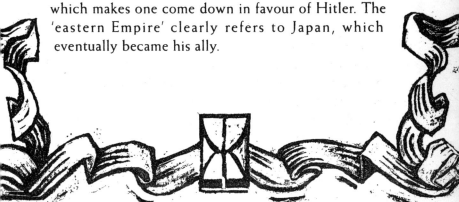

HITLER

Wild and hungry beasts will cross rivers.
The greatest battles shall be against Hi$ter.
He will cause great men to be dragged in a cage of iron,
When this son of Germany respects no law.

(CENTURY 2 – QUATRAIN 24)

This is one of Nostradamus's most famous quatrains, mainly because he mentions Hitler by name. True, the spelling is marginally inaccurate, but it would be hard to conceive that the prophet was describing anyone other than the Führer – 'the son of Germany who respects no law'.

What is also important about this quatrain, as Erika Cheetham points out in her book, *Further Prophecies of Nostradamus*, is the dangerous self-fulfilling quality of some prophecies. Hitler was deeply fascinated by astrology and the occult and was fully versed in the work of Nostradamus. There must have been a great temptation for a man with his rampant ego to attempt to make them come true.

THE KRAFFT QUATRAIN

**The people gathered to see a new sight,
Leaders and the King among the onlookers.
Pillars and walls will fall, but as if by a miracle,
The King and thirty others will be saved.**

(CENTURY 6 – QUATRAIN 51)

So deep-seated was the Nazi hierarchy's belief in astrology and the occult that they retained the services of one of Europe's leading astrologers, Ernst Krafft, a Swiss citizen and fervent supporter of the Nazi Party. Krafft was attached to Goebbels's Propaganda Ministry as a 'consultant'. At the beginning of November 1939, Krafft submitted a paper to Goebbels in which he used the above quatrain, together with astrological calculations, to predict an assassination attempt against the Führer some time between the seventh and the tenth of that month. Hitler had expressly forbidden predictions which concerned him personally and so the document was locked away in a safe.

Two days after Krafft submitted his report, Hitler was addressing a public meeting. The Führer was due to speak for an hour, but was called away on urgent business and left early, together with several other Nazi leaders. Minutes after their departure, a bomb, which had been placed behind a pillar, exploded and killed several people.

HITLER AND MUSSOLINI

**The Roman's power will be totally usurped,
After imitating the example of his mighty neighbour.
Occult hatreds and disputes,
Will push back the follies of these idiots.**

(CENTURY 3 – QUATRAIN 63)

The Roman in the first line of this quatrain is, of course, Benito Mussolini, who made the fatal mistake of attempting to emulate the style and ambitions of his more 'mighty neighbour', Adolf Hitler.

The third line again reminds us of Hitler's fascination with the occult. Many historians believe that this obsession lay behind some of the more bizarre and inexplicable military decisions he made during the course of the war, most particularly his decision to send his troops into a Russian winter; it also prompted him to call a premature halt to the effective V2 rocket campaign.

Hitler was not alone in his obsession with the occult. Goebbels, influenced by his wife, actually introduced the Führer to the subject, while Heinrich Himmler commandeered some of the finest academic minds in Germany to research the esoteric properties of top hats, as worn by Etonians, believing that they, together with Eton's bells, were somehow deflecting the Luftwaffe bombs. And the idea for Rudolph Hess's bizarre flight to Scotland came to him in a dream.

RISE OF THE NAZIS

Various factions will spring up in Germany,
Greatly reminiscent of paganism,
But their slavish nature and slender resources,
Will make them despoiled in return.

(CENTURY 3 – QUATRAIN 76)

In this quatrain, Nostradamus predicts the emergence of the Nazi party and its many offshoots, such as the SA, the Youth Association of the Nazi Party, the SS, the Hitler Youth and the Gestapo.

The return to 'paganism' refers to the fact that religious marriage ceremonies were replaced by ritualised wedding rites. During the proceedings, which were overseen by an SS leader, gifts of bread and salt were exchanged along with rings.

MEIN KAMPF A RECIPE FOR NAZISM

Under the guise of delivering his people from servitude,
He will himself usurp the people's power.
He will wreak the worst by trickery with the aid of a new republic,
Using the text in the struggle, the false ideas of his book.

(CENTURY 5 – QUATRAIN 5)

After their ill-conceived putsch in 1923, the National Socialist Party was banned and Hitler was condemned to five years imprisonment, though he served less than a year in Landsberg Prison.

He used his time there to write the first volume of *Mein Kampf*, which would form the cornerstone of Nazi doctrine.

The book's publication in Munich in 1925 coincided with the National Socialists' rebirth under Hitler's leadership. Five years later, the Nazi party boasted 107 deputies and in 1933, the party achieved outright power in Germany.

A GROWING THREAT

The Bird of Prey, flying to the window,
Before conflict with the French, makes his preparations.
Some will take him as good, some as evil.
The little party will take him as a good omen.

(CENTURY 1 – QUATRAIN 34)

The 'Bird of Prey' in the first line of the quatrain could as easily apply to either Napoleon or Hitler. It was a metaphor adopted by Nostradamus to describe both, and both in turn adopted the eagle as their insignia. Later lines in the verse, however, make it more likely that the subject in question is Hitler.

The image of the 'Bird of Prey flying to the window' describes Hitler's expansionist intentions in the 1930s and the threat perceived by those countries that were less inclined to a policy of appeasement, notably France and England. When Nostradamus talks about Hitler making his preparations, he is presumably referring to his annexation of first Austria, then Czechoslovakia and Poland, before his confrontation with France.

Today, Hitler is universally portrayed as the personification of evil. This was not the case, however, in his own time. In the early years of his rule, he was widely considered, both inside and outside Germany, as the country's salvation. As Nostradamus says, opinions were deeply divided.

The last line of the quatrain clearly refers to the embryonic Nazi Party, which was a tiny right-wing fringe group when Hitler joined in 1923. Its members soon saw him as a potential leader, not only of their party but of a greater Germany.

ULTIMATE POWER

He, like Claudius, will not have the power to rule Germany,
But will achieve as much by seduction,
Using short speeches and long,
He will bring about the planned action against the
government.

(CENTURY 6 – QUATRAIN 84)

This is a typical use of simile by Nostradamus, as he draws a direct comparison between Hitler and the Emperor Claudius of Ancient Rome. Both men initially operated from a weak base; as a child, Claudius was frail and sickly, while Hitler came from a humble background and his launching pad for power in Germany was a beer cellar in Munich. Both men went on to rule their respective `empires' for thirteen years.

The much ridiculed Claudius proceeded to conquer England, the Rhine, Austria, Armenia, the Balkans and parts of Africa. At home, he overcame several attempts to usurp his power.

Hitler also achieved absolute power slowly and gradually. In January 1933, he agreed to form a government. From there he became dictator in three stages. First, he dissolved the existing Reichstag and formed a new one, awarding himself sweeping powers. Next, in 1934, he ridded himself of all potential opposition in the infamous 'Night of the Long Knives'. Finally, he declared himself Führer.

MISCELLANEOUS QUATRAINS

Most of Nostradamus' quatrains pertaining to the years between the two wars concentrated on the political affairs of mainland Europe, but he did turn his attention to a number of other, isolated incidents. One in particular, the abdication of King Edward VIII, demonstrates his genius for prophecy.

THE ABDICATION OF EDWARD VIII

In two of his most famous quatrains, Nostradamus predicted the abdication of King Edward VIII four hundred years before it actually happened. If the interpretation of some of the prophet's predictions might appear somewhat obscure, nothing could be more obvious and straightforward than these.

> **A young man, born to rule Britain,**
> **Will be entrusted by his dying father.**
> **The latter dead, the former will cause controversy in**
> **London.**
> **And from the son, the throne will be demanded.**

(CENTURY 10 – QUATRAIN 40)

When King George V died in 1936, his eldest son, Edward, Prince of Wales, automatically succeeded him. Edward was a bachelor and something of a playboy, a role considered befitting a Prince but not a King. Among Edward's many female friends was Mrs Wallis Simpson, an American divorcee, now married to one of the Prince's friends. A few days after the old King's death, Mrs Simpson started divorce proceedings against her second husband,

and Edward announced his intention of marrying her. Parliament tried to dissuade him, but he was adamant. Finally they were forced to send him an ultimatum give up Mrs Simpson or give up the throne. Edward chose the latter course and on 10 December, 1936, millions of British subjects heard him announce his abdication over the radio. He was given the title of the Duke of Windsor and left the country to spend the rest of his life in exile. The irony of the whole abdication scandal was that Edward could well have had his cake and eaten it. He could have married a suitable consort and continued his relationship with Mrs Simpson. Royal mistresses were the norm at that time and were tolerated, provided the affairs were conducted with discretion.

After refusing to accept that a divorce is unsuitable,
The King of the Isles will be considered as unworthy.
He will be driven out by force,
And one will take his place who has no mark of kingship.

(CENTURY 10 – QUATRAIN 22)

This quatrain is almost identical to the previous one, except for the last line where Nostradamus describes Edward's replacement as having 'no mark of kingship.' This is perhaps a little harsh. It is true that George VI had a terrible stammer and was very shy, but to be fair to him, he had never expected to become king and had not been groomed for the role.

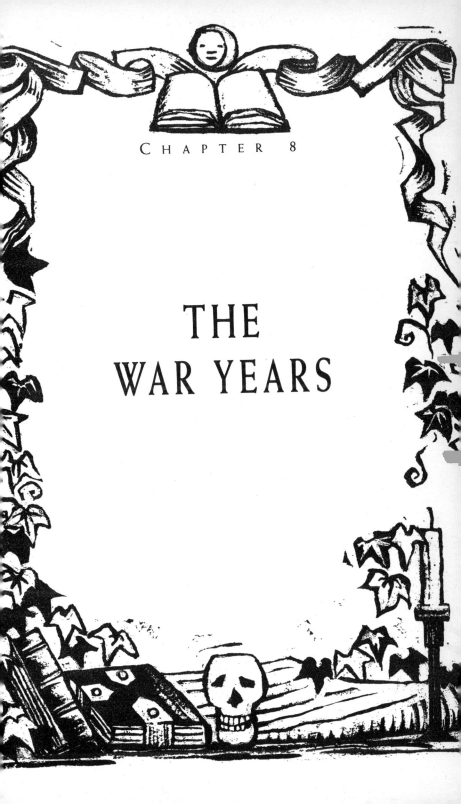

CHAPTER 8

THE
WAR YEARS

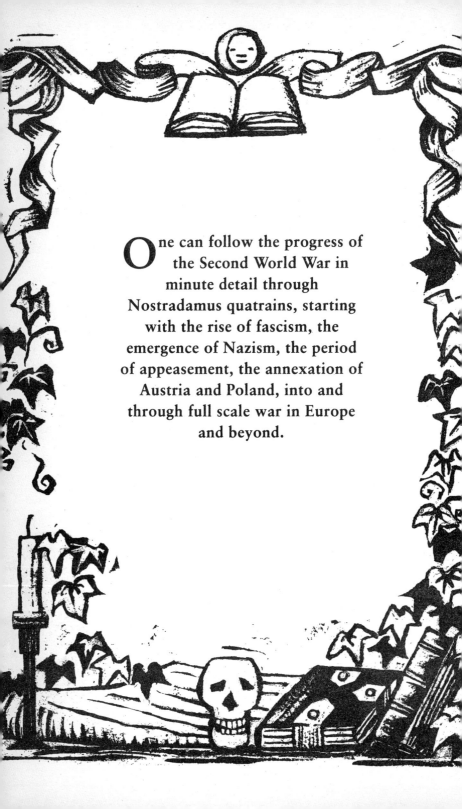

One can follow the progress of the Second World War in minute detail through Nostradamus quatrains, starting with the rise of fascism, the emergence of Nazism, the period of appeasement, the annexation of Austria and Poland, into and through full scale war in Europe and beyond.

JAW-JAW

After experiencing the horrors of the First World War, most sane people in Western Europe had no desire to repeat the experience and so, despite the obvious threat from Hitler's Germany, government after government signed a series of treaties and pacts in a vain attempt to avoid armed conflict.

THE 1938 DECLARATION

**The Eagle, following the announced decision,
Will honour the French before the war.
One party will take him in good faith,
One on the left will be suspicious. The weaker will resist.**

(CENTURY 1 – QUATRAIN 34)

In 1938, the Russians and Germans seemed set upon peace between their two countries, despite what happened in the rest of Europe. They were anxious to reassure Britain and France, the two other most powerful nations in Europe, of their sincerity. In this quatrain, Nostradamus rightly predicts the differing reactions to the status quo.

THE MUNICH AGREEMENT

A dreadful and undignified infamy,
Will follow the act upon which they congratulate themselves.
It is only a pretext, without goodwill,
To the point where Britain will not remain at peace.

(CENTURY 7 – QUATRAIN 90)

This quatrain could apply to any one of the peace treaties signed between 1938 and 1939.

On 6 December 1938 Ribbentrop and Bonnet signed a Franco-German declaration at the Quai d'Orsay, in which both agreed to respect one another's national sovereignty, and Germany renounced its long-held claims over the French territories of Alsace and Lorraine.

In the same year, a similar, and equally hollow document was signed by the pacifist British Prime Minister Neville Chamberlain. It was he that returned from Europe, proudly brandishing the Anglo-German declaration, and announced, 'Peace in our time'. His enthusiasm for the treaty was not shared by many of his colleagues, and within a matter of months he had been forced to agree to a massive rearmament program and the re-introduction of compulsory military service. In September 1939, Hitler invaded Poland, in direct contradiction to his assurances, and, as Nostradamus predicted, Britain immediately declared war.

GERMAN-SOVIET PACT

**Great numbers will be condemned,
When the monarchs are reconciled.
But one of them will be so embarrassed and damaged,
That they will hardly remain allies.**

(CENTURY 2 – QUATRAIN 38)

In this quatrain, Nostradamus predicts the outcome of the Non-Aggression Pact signed between Hitler and Stalin in 1939. The agreement suited the USSR because, at the very least, it bought the country some time in which to re-arm. Stalin would have been wise to have read *Mein Kampf* more carefully, because in it Hitler spells out his intentions for Europe quite specifically. His aim was always to defeat France and Britain and then to turn East and overthrow the communist regime.

Like other European leaders before him, Stalin continued to be reassured by Hitler's promises of non-aggression, totally ignoring intelligence reports that German troops were massing on his borders. Sure enough, less than two years after signing his pact with Russia, Hitler launched an army of three million men and more than three thousand tanks against the Soviets.

WINSTON CHURCHILL

**The great Bulldog, isolated from parliament,
Will be angered by a strange alliance.
After defeating Poland,
The wolf and the bear will defy each other.**

(CENTURY 5 – QUATRAIN 4)

In this quatrain, the 'great Bulldog' is generally considered to be a reference to Winston Churchill. For years he had urged parliament to rearm in readiness for German aggression. His words had fallen on deaf ears. He was indeed angered by a strange alliance, in fact more than one. He had absolutely no faith in any of the treaties signed with Hitler.

In this same quatrain, Nostradamus accurately predicts the invasion of Poland. On 9 December 1939, the German army – 'the wolf' – attacked Warsaw. A week later, the Russian army – 'the bear' – crossed Poland's eastern border and, in accordance with the German-Russian pact, they divided the country.

Initially, Hitler seemed true to his word, but, on 21 June 1941, determined to drive the Communists out of Europe, he ordered the Wehrmacht to launch its attack on the Russian army.

THE MAGINOT LINE

**Near the great river, a vast earth ditch will be dug.
It will be divided by water into fifteen sections.
The city will be taken, with much blood and fire.
And the great majority will be involved in the conflict.**

(CENTURY 4 – QUATRAIN 80)

In this quatrain, Nostradamus appears not only to have predicted the nature and consequences of the Franco-German conflict, but also the strategies employed within it.

Plans for the Maginot Line, a vast defensive wall running along France's eastern border with Germany, dated back to the 1920s. It was eventually completed in 1934, and stretched from Longwy to the Swiss border, broken in fifteen places by rivers. Vastly expensive, but unquestionably a masterpiece of civil engineering, it comprised a series of self-sufficient fortresses, each dug seven storeys underground, which were connected by an underground railway system. The French Government were confident that it rendered the country impregnable from the East. Unfortunately, they were wrong, and for the most part, the invading Germans skirted round it.

It is possible that this is yet another case where those in power used Nostradamus' quatrains as guidance, and the line might never have been built at all had it not been for this particular prediction. James Laver suggests that, in the 19th Century, Abbé Torne used this particular verse as his basis to warn that the next German invasion of France would come through Switzerland.

The Abbé and his followers would have been well advised to study the last two lines of the quatrain more carefully. They leave the reader in little doubt that the Line was doomed to failure and, as a result of this, Paris – 'the city' – would fall.

WAR-WAR

THE INVASION OF HOLLAND, BELGIUM AND FRANCE

When the great one carries off the prize of Nuremberg,
Of Augsburg, and of Basel;
Frankfurt retaken by the leader of Cologne.
He will go through Flanders, right into the heart of France.

(CENTURY 3 – QUATRAIN 53)

In this quatrain, Nostradamus describes Hitler's triumphs leading up to and during the early stages of the Second World War.

The reference to Nuremberg in the first line describes the Führer's great rallies in that city in 1933 and 1934, the platform from which he launched his expansionist plans. Augsburg, Frankfurt and Cologne allform part of the Rhineland, which Hitler annexed.

In the last line of the quatrain, Nostradamus describes the first stage of Germany's invasion of France, which began on 10 May 1940 with an attack launched from the west, through Belgium and Holland – 'Flanders'.

PARIS FALLS

Under the guise of piety,
The country will be attacked by enemies through treachery.
While people thought they were sleeping in safety,
The troops in Liege will march across Belgium.

(CENTURY 6 – QUATRAIN 30)

Despite the Ribbentrop-Bonnet pact, signed at the Quai d'Orsay in 1938, the German Army attacked the Netherlands and France on 10 May 1940. Their first success was the destruction of the Dutch and Belgian defences. Two days later they swept across the Ardennes and the French frontier. On 5 June, the Wehrmacht resumed their offensive on the Somme and pushed south. Eleven days later they were in Paris.

THE OCCUPATION OF FRANCE

The French government will be greatly altered.
The empire will be transferred to another country.
They will be subjected to new ways and new laws.
Those who came through Rouen and Chartres will
wreak havoc.

(CENTURY 3 – QUATRAIN 49)

As Nostradamus predicted, the French government was greatly changed after German occupation. The Nazis supported the puppet government of the defeatist Marshal Pétain, whose only answer to his country's predicament was to negotiate an armistice. France's only hope lay in England – 'another country' – in the person of General de Gaulle.

PÉTAIN AND THE VICHY REGIME

> The old man is derided and robbed of his power,
> By the foreigner who will be severe with him.
> The hands of his sons are consumed before him.
> He will betray his brothers at Chartres, Orléans and Rouen.

(CENTURY 4 – QUATRAIN 61)

This is the first of three quatrains in which Nostradamus describes Marshal Pétain and his collaborators in most unflattering terms. After the German invasion of France in 1940, Pétain – his nickname was 'the old man' – negotiated an armistice with Hitler. His aim was to live alongside his German occupiers and thereby stay out of the broader war. Hitler – 'the foreigner' – immediately broke all the conditions of the agreement and, in 1942, took overall control of the country, leaving Pétain an object of derision among all French patriots.

After the liberation of France, Pétain was tried and sentenced to death for treason. This was later commuted to life imprisonment on the Ile d'Yeu, where he died in 1951.

> The old man disappointed in his main hope,
> Another will attain the leadership of his country.
> He will hold power for twenty months with great force,
> A great tyrant leaving worse behind him.

(CENTURY 8 – QUATRAIN 65)

In this quatrain, the 'old man' again refers to Marshal Pétain, whose hopes of a genuine armistice were dashed. The one who seized control from him was, of course, Hitler. France was occupied by the Germans on 11 November 1942. The Normandy landings commenced on 6 June, 1944 – nineteen months and twenty-five days later. Nostradamus was out by six days!

> The old man, trembling,
> Will pressure not to give up the captives.
> The old, not so old, speaking timidly,
> To free his friends in a lawful manner.

(CENTURY 10 – QUATRAIN 85)

This is yet another derisory description of Pétain by Nostradamus. In this quatrain he is referring to the his pathetic attempts to negotiate with the German occupiers to stop them using French civilians as slave labourers.

DE GAULLE IN EXILE

The change will be truly difficult.
Both the city and province will benefit by it.
A wise man of distinguished rank will be chased out by a
cunning one.
By land and sea, people will change the estate.

(CENTURY 4 – QUATRAIN 21)

In this quatrain, Nostradamus is describing the wartime life of
General Charles de Gaulle – 'the wise man of distinguished rank'.
His exile in London – 'the change' – must indeed have been difficult,
but through his efforts, Paris – 'the city' – did eventually benefit.

The last line of the quatrain 'by land and sea', presumably refers
to the Normandy landings and the subsequent battle to free
France from German occupation.

A TERRIBLE COST

The people of Marseilles will change totally;
Pursued, they flee as far as Lyons,
Narbonne and Toulouse, angered by Bordeaux.
The killed and imprisoned will number almost a million.

(CENTURY 1 – QUATRAIN 72)

When the German army marched into Paris in 1940, the French Government fled to Vichy, where they remained nominally in control of southern and western France until the end of 1942, when British successes in North Africa encouraged the Germans to tighten their grip on France. Narbonne, Toulouse and Lyons were three French cities which were under the direct control of the Vichy regime – 'Bordeaux' – a situation which angered them. Marseilles was under German occupation, a no more appetising situation. In the last line, Nostradamus is referring to France's war dead, which numbered almost seven hundred thousand.

THE BATTLE OF BRITAIN

The island people having been besieged for a long time,
Will unleash terrible violence against their enemies.
Those abroad, overcome, will die of hunger,
Such starvation has never been seen.

(CENTURY 3 – QUATRAIN 71)

The 'island people' referred to in this quatrain are the British. After the fall of France in the summer of 1940, Britain was forced to fight the might of the German armies almost single-handed for more than a year. Later in the war, in reprisal, the RAF mounted massive bombing raids on German cities. These indiscriminate and controversial attacks caused more than a million German civilian casualties.

As in many Nostradamus quatrains, this verse describes two quite separate aspects of the same subject. In the last two lines, 'those abroad who die of hunger', refers to Hitler's systematic extermination of Jews, gypsies, Russians and others the Nazis considered 'undesirable'. More than 13 million died in all, many by the gas chamber, but more by maltreatment and malnutrition. It is also possible that this refers to British soldiers captured by the Japanese, many of whom also died of malnutrition.

DOG FIGHTS

They will think they have seen the sun at night,
When they see the half-pig, half-man.
Noise, screams, battles fought in the sky.
The brute beasts will be heard talking.

(CENTURY 1 – QUATRAIN 64)

This quatrain takes some untangling, but it appears to describe an aerial dog fight. Anyone on the ground would see the flashes and explosions lighting up the night sky, as fighters attacked bombers with machine guns, and bombers unleashed their cargoes. 'Half-man, half-pig' describes vividly the profile of a pilot wearing his helmet, goggles and oxygen mask. The 'noise' and 'screams' would be the weaponry and the high-pitched engines of the fighters, and the 'brute beasts talking' could refer to pilots communicating with one another over the radio.

PEARL HARBOR

A naval force will be overcome at night.
Fire in the ruins of the ships of the West,
A new disguise in the great coloured ships,
Fury from the vanquished, and victory in the mist.

(CENTURY 9 – QUATRAIN 100)

The most logical interpretation of this quatrain is that it describes the Japanese attack on Pearl Harbor in the early morning of 7 December 1941. The attack was launched without warning, or any formal declaration of war. The Japanese air force damaged 19 American naval vessels, destroying six battleships, and wrecked more than 100 aircraft on the ground. More than 3,000 Americans were killed. This single attack brought the United States into the Second World War.

THE LIBERATION OF ITALY

Milan, Ferrar, Turin, Aquilia,
Capua and Brindisi will be harassed by the French,
By the British and the army of the eagle,
When the old British general will hold Rome.

(CENTURY 5 – QUATRAIN 99)

In this quatrain, Nostradamus predicts the allied advance through Italy following the Sicily landings and the capture of Rome. The 'British general' who held Rome was, of course, Field Marshal Montgomery, who headed the allied forces as they entered the capital on 4 June, 1944. The 'army of the eagle' is that of the USA.

THE NORMANDY LANDINGS

**With machines of both water and land,
Through the sheer number of their attacks,
This mixture of foreigners will be both thrilling
and horrifying,
And soon they will strike at the enemy, from the sea
up to the cliffs.**

(CENTURY 1 – QUATRAIN 29)

This is one of Nostradamus's most impressive wartime quatrains. It captures not only the detail, but also the atmosphere of the Normandy landings on 6 June 1944. The sight of the massive allied force landing on the beaches, with their armada of amphibious tanks and landing craft – 'machines of both water and land' – must indeed have been thrilling for the French, and terrifying for the Germans.

THE FALL OF THE THIRD REICH

**The new empire will be desolated,
And undergo changes because of the northern forces.
From Sicily they will be chased,
And Philippe's support will be undermined.**

(CENTURY 8 – QUATRAIN 81)

In this quatrain, Nostradamus sees the Third Reich – 'the new empire' – under attack on all fronts, and its downfall must inevitably follow.

For two years after the abortive invasion of Russia, a vast German army was committed to the Eastern front. Then, in 1943, the Afrika Korps suffered defeat in North Africa, and this was followed by the allied landings in Sicily and their advance into mainland Italy. Even in France, Hitler's puppet, Philipe Pétain had been undermined by the French people. The end was inevitable.

THE DEATH OF THE FÜHRER

**The fortress of those under siege,
Was cut into the depths with gunpowder.
The traitor will be entombed in it.
Never was there so terrible a schism among the Germans.**

(CENTURY 4 – QUATRAIN 40)

The last weeks of Hitler's life were spent in a concrete bunker in the grounds of the Berlin Chancellory. By this time, the war was hopelessly lost, but the Führer continued to plan and order grandiose military operations. Finally, surrounded by a handful of stoic followers and aware of the advancing allies, even he was forced to face defeat. He could not, however, face the humiliation of capture. He married his mistress, Eva Braun, and then, to the best of our knowledge, she took poison while Hitler shot himself.

The 'terrible schism' described by Nostradamus in the last line of the quatrain is the partition of Germany when the post-war map of Europe was redrawn.

WAR CRIMES

THE HOLOCAUST

The first man of the Third will do worse than Nero,
He will be as ferocious in draining as in shedding human
blood.
He will cause ovens to be built.
The empire will end, and he will cause great scandal.

(CENTURY 9 – QUATRAIN 17)

By the early 1940s, the Allies were already well aware that the Germans were perpetrating all manner of atrocities, but it was not until their forces pushed deep into German-occupied Europe that they realised the appalling scale of the genocide.

From the beginning, the Nazi regime had deprived Jews, gypsies and other ethnic and social minorities of their civil rights. Soon they were being interned, tortured and murdered. In January 1942, as Germany gained control of mainland Europe, the Nazi leadership held a meeting to establish their plan for the 'final solution'. Jews and other 'undesirables' were herded into concentration camps and systematically murdered or worked to death. By the end of the war, more than six million European Jews – out of a population of eight million – had perished. Nostradamus not only foresaw the mass slaughter, he also described the manner in which it would be perpetrated.

THE OVENS

The new Nero will hurl into three ovens
Young people and burn them alive.
Happy are they that are away from such acts.
Three of his countrymen will spy on him to kill him.

(CENTURY 9 – QUATRAIN 53)

This second quatrain dealing with the Nazi death camps is even more graphic than the first, and also includes another element in the Hitler saga. The last line refers to his 'countrymen' planning to kill him. Towards the end of the war, there were numerous plots against his life, the most famous of which was headed by General Beck and Colonel von Stauffenberg. They placed a bomb under Hitler's desk at his headquarters on 20 July 1944. The device exploded, but Hitler escaped with only minor injuries. The conspirators were rounded up and summarily executed.

THE NUREMBERG TRIALS AND THE COLD WAR

There will be a great number of people condemned,
When the heads of state are reconciled.
But one of them will create trouble,
And those that waged war together will no longer be allies.

(CENTURY 2 – QUATRAIN 38)

In the first line of this quatrain, Nostradamus is anticipating the Nuremberg trials, which commenced on 20 November 1945. Twenty-four German military and political leaders stood accused of 'crimes against humanity'. For the first and last time the four allied powers – Great Britain, France, the United States and the USSR – stood united in their condemnation of Nazi atrocities. It was a brief respite, however, and the Cold War was soon upon us.

CHAPTER 9

IN OUR
OWN TIME

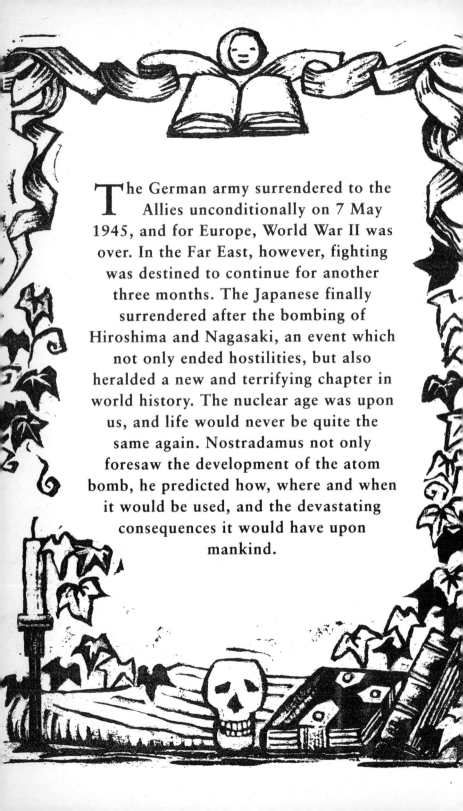

The German army surrendered to the Allies unconditionally on 7 May 1945, and for Europe, World War II was over. In the Far East, however, fighting was destined to continue for another three months. The Japanese finally surrendered after the bombing of Hiroshima and Nagasaki, an event which not only ended hostilities, but also heralded a new and terrifying chapter in world history. The nuclear age was upon us, and life would never be quite the same again. Nostradamus not only foresaw the development of the atom bomb, he predicted how, where and when it would be used, and the devastating consequences it would have upon mankind.

Nuclear warfare was by far the most important of Nostradamus' prophecies for the late twentieth century, but it was certainly not the only one. In this section you will find quatrains which predict events as diverse as the Hungarian uprising, the Apollo space mission, the career of Mao Tse Tung and the Kennedy assassinations. Nostradamus also predicts the beginning of World War III, and the rise of a third antichrist, Mabus, from out of the East.

Nostradamus's own world centred around France and its immediate neighbours and his quatrains up to this period have generally focused on events within that arena. As we move forward in time, however, his horizons widen and his predictions encompass the entire globe. It is as if his foresight developed in parallel with today's technology, and the world for him became a smaller and more accessible place.

THE NUCLEAR NIGHTMARE

The nuclear age began, in fact, in Germany in 1938, when scientists confirmed what physicists had long proposed, that nuclear fission was possible. By splitting the atom untold quantities of energy could be released, energy which promised limitless power, power which could be harnessed for constructive or destructive purposes. There is little doubt that Hitler would have had nuclear weapons years ahead of the Americans had it not been for his anti-Semitic policies. Most of Germany's top scientists were Jewish and fled to the United States in the late

1930s, taking their secrets with them. In December 1938, a group of these refugee scientists, led by Albert Einstein, addressed a letter to President Roosevelt, explaining their theories and their fears that Hitler intended to use their work for destructive purposes. The President immediately established the Manhattan Project, whose brief was to ensure that, if nuclear weapons were to become a reality, the USA would have them first.

A team of top physicists and scientists, under the leadership of J. Robert Oppenheimer, spent the next five years at a purpose-built laboratory at Los Alamos, New Mexico, turning theory into practice. On 16 July 1945, their dream – or nightmare – was realised at Alamogordo, with the explosion of the world's first atomic bomb. It surpassed the theorists' wildest expectations, producing energy more than a million times greater than the equivalent weight of TNT.

Less than four weeks after that initial explosion, the atom bomb was deployed in the theatre of war. Four hundred years earlier, the prophet Nostradamus foresaw it all; the power, and its terrible consequences.

THE BOMB

As the sun rises, a great fire will be seen,
Noise and light extending towards the north.
Within the globe is death and screams.
Death awaits through the weapon, fire and plague.

(CENTURY 2 – QUATRAIN 91)

In this quatrain, Nostradamus not only describes the awful power of the atom bomb, but anticipates the long term consequences of its deployment. The word 'plague' in the last line undoubtedly refers to the appalling physical effects of radiation. The symptoms of extreme radiation poisoning – suppurating sores, swollen limbs and blackened skin – are not unlike those which Nostradamus must have encountered on countless occasions during his time as a plague doctor.

HIROSHIMA AND NAGASAKI

Close by two harbours, and within two cities,
There will be two scourges, worse than has ever been seen.
Hunger, plague, and people dispossessed by war.
They will plead for help from Almighty God.

(CENTURY 2 – QUATRAIN 6)

The United States Air Force dropped atomic bombs on the two Japanese cities of Hiroshima and Nagasaki on 6 August and 9 August 1945. Both cities were destroyed. More than 100,000 civilians died immediately; countless thousands more died agonising deaths in the weeks and months that followed.

As Nostradamus predicted, the first, and as yet last nuclear attacks were directed at two 'harbour' cities, and these attacks were indeed followed by 'hunger and plague'. The hunger was caused by the total destruction of the cities' municipal services and infrastructure. Water was undrinkable, and food inedible. The 'plague' covers a mass of illnesses and injuries which were caused by radiation poisoning.

A CHANGING WORLD

The decade after World War II saw an unprecedented upheaval in world politics. The map of Europe was redrawn; occupied nations fought to re-establish their identities; new nations were born, old ones divided or reunited; and great leaders – some good some bad – came to the forefront. Nostradamus predicted many of these events with great clarity.

THE STATE OF ISRAEL

**Newcomers build a home without defences,
Occupying land which was previously uninhabitable.
Meadows, houses, and towns to be taken with pleasure.
Famine, war and sickness will be on this land for a long time.**

(CENTURY 2 – QUATRAIN 19)

The 'newcomers' in this quatrain are the Jewish survivors of the Nazi Holocaust who, in 1948, established their own state in Palestine. Their presence was resented by disenfranchised Palestinians and their other Arab neighbours. From its inception, Israel was always vulnerable to attack from all quarters. Indeed, there were a succession of Arab-Israeli wars in 1948, 1956, 1967, 1973 and 1982, several of which Nostradamus predicted – 'famine, war and sickness will be on this land for a long time'. Initially, the State of Israel might have been 'without defences', but it was a situation that was soon rectified.

In the second line of the quatrain, Nostradamus describes the land as 'previously uninhabitable'. This is something of an exaggeration – Palestinians were already living there – but in 1948, it was certainly no more than an arid stretch of desert, which the Israelis transformed by dint of hard work and foreign aid.

THE SIX DAYS' WAR

By a new law, new territories will be occupied,
Towards Syria, Jordan and Palestine.
A great Arab power will be destroyed,
Before the Summer Solstice.

(CENTURY 3 – QUATRAIN 97)

The Six Days War started on 5 June, 1967, and ended on 10 June, as Nostradamus predicted, 'before the Summer Solstice', which falls on 21 June.

At dawn on the first day of the war, the Israeli air force launched a surprise attack against Egypt – 'a great Arab power' – Most of the Egyptian air force was wiped out, and their army was in disarray within a few hours of the commencement of hostilities. The Israelis drove across the Sinai Desert virtually unopposed, until they reached the Suez Canal. They also attacked Jordan and, despite fierce opposition, succeeded in occupying the ancient holy city of Jerusalem.

When terms of peace were being negotiated, the Israelis refused to return much of the territory they had occupied, claiming that it provided essential protection for their country against Arab aggression. A compromise – 'a new law' – was reached which allowed Israel to stay in the Golan Heights, the West Bank, South Lebanon and the Gaza Strip – 'new territories'.

POST-WAR FRANCE

It would be almost inconceivable for Nostradamus not to have made mention of the fate of his beloved France during this period, and indeed he did. In one remarkable quatrain, he describes the return of General Charles De Gaulle from exile in England and his rise to power.

DE GAULLE

Hercules, king of Rome and Annemarc,
Three times the leader will be called De Gaulle.
Italy will tremble and the waters of St Mark.
The first above all kings to be honoured.

(CENTURY 9 – QUATRAIN 33)

The first and third line of this quatrain are somewhat obscure, but the second and fourth could not be more straightforward.

Charles de Gaulle first came to prominence in 1940, when his tank division put up a spirited defence against the advancing German army. He was appointed Under Secretary for War on 5 June, 1940, but fled to Britain a week later when he realised that defeat was inevitable. On 18 June, he radioed from London, imploring the French people to resist occupation at all costs. He was immediately condemned to death in absentia by Marshal Pétain's Vichy government. Despite this, de Gaulle spent the remainder of the war building and coordinating the activities of the Free French resistance forces. In 1943, he formed a provisional government in exile in readiness for the impending liberation of France.

After the Normandy invasion and the liberation of Paris, de Gaulle became the President of the newly formed Fourth Republic. In 1946, after two years of internal party squabbling, he was forced to resign. He returned to power in 1958 by popular demand, as President of the Fifth Republic. In doing so, de Gaulle fulfilled Nostradamus's prophecy. He was indeed 'three times leader'; President of the Provisional Government in exile, President of the Fourth Republic and President of the Fifth Republic.

Even the last line of the quatrain is borne out. There is no question that his standing on the world political stage was infinitely greater than that of any of the old kings of France.

CHAIRMAN MAO

In keeping with the new, intercontinental nature of his prophecies, Nostradamus looked east and predicted the life and career of another of the world's great leaders, Mao Tse Tung.

> Remote from this kingdom, sent on a perilous journey,
> He will lead a great army and keep it for himself.
> The King will hold his nation to ransom.
> With his revolution, he will pillage the entire country.

(CENTURY 8 – QUATRAIN 92)

Mao Tse Tung was born in 1893 in China's Hunan province which was indeed 'remote from Nostradamus's kingdom – France.

At the age of 27, after studying classics in Beijing, Mao returned to Hunan and became a founding member and regional leader of the budding Chinese Communist Party. The party grew rapidly, but in 1927 General Chiang Kai Shek reversed his Nationalist Party's policy and purged all Communists from positions of power. Mao fled to the countryside, and there formed the Chinese Soviet, electing himself as chairman. He raised a peasant army and waged a 'people's war' against the Nationalists using guerrilla tactics, harassing the government forces for seven years before Chiang Kai Shek's army finally pinned him down. Rather than surrendering, however, Mao 'led his army' on a six thousand mile march – 'a perilous journey' – through the Chinese interior to Shensi, a feat of courage and endurance which has since become known as the 'Long March'.

As Nostradamus predicted, Mao remained absolute commander of the exiled Communist army – he kept it for himself – and ten years later, in 1946, he embarked on an all-out war with the Nationalists. Well-trained and well-armed, the new Communist army finally defeated the Nationalists in 1949. Chiang Kai Shek and his followers fled to Taiwan, and Mao set up the People's Republic of China, with himself as Chairman.

By the end of the 1950s, Mao had established himself as a demi-God and absolute ruler of mainland China. His regime was repressive. He deliberately set out to destroy the traditional family structure by herding the people into communes, and sought to control their thoughts as well as their actions through the pages of his Little Red Book – 'the King will hold his nation to ransom'.

THE HUNGARIAN UPRISING

**Through life and death the rule of Hungary will change.
The law will become more harsh than slavery.
The great city will echo with cries and laments.
Castor and Pollux are enemies in the field.**

(CENTURY 2 – QUATRAIN 90)

213

This is one of the least ambiguous of all the prophecies of Nostradamus. It refers to the Hungarian uprising of 1956.

On 1 November 1956, the Hungarian people, tired of Soviet tyranny, demanded the return of their independence. On behalf of his people, Premier Imre Nagy renounced the Warsaw Pact. There were celebrations in the streets of Budapest, but the euphoria was short-lived. Three days later, Russian tanks rolled across the Hungarian border and into the capital. The Hungarian crowds took to the streets again, but this time, rather than celebrating, they were hurling Molotov cocktails at the invading army. Despite pleas to the West for help, the uprising was quickly quashed and Premier Nagy and thousands of his supporters were executed by Russian firing squads.

In the last line of this quatrain, Nostradamus mentions the classical twins 'Castor and Pollux'. This has a double meaning. On the one hand it refers to pro- and anti-Communist Hungarian brothers who fought against one another during the uprising; on the other it refers to the twin cities of Buda and Pest.

THE KENNEDY DYNASTY

Nostradamus wrote almost a thousand quatrains in his *Centuries*, but there is no doubt that five of these did more to bring his work to the attention of a mass contemporary audience than all the rest put together. They concern the Kennedy clan, and more specifically the assassination of President John Kennedy and his younger brother, Senator Robert Kennedy.

John F Kennedy was elected 35th President of the United States in 1960. At 43, he was the youngest man ever elected to that office. He was also the first Roman Catholic. Handsome, charismatic, vastly wealthy and extremely popular with young America, he looked set for a brilliant political career. When that was over, the Kennedy clan could offer two younger, but equally charismatic brothers to fill his shoes. America was set for a dynasty. But, as Nostradamus predicted, it was all destined to end in tragedy.

JOHN F KENNEDY

Before the battle, the great man will fall.
The great one to death, death too quickly and grieved.
Born imperfect, he will go a great part of the way.
Near the river of blood, the earth stained.

(CENTURY 2 – QUATRAIN 57)

It is unclear precisely to which 'battle' Nostradamus is referring. Perhaps he is saying that Kennedy died without witnessing the misery and humiliation of Vietnam, or even that he might have prevented it, but there is no denying that 'the great man' went to his death too quickly and was 'grieved'.

Nostradamus goes on to describe Kennedy as 'born imperfect'. This again is accurate. John F Kennedy suffered from Addison's disease and had a lower back disorder which troubled him all his life.

However, the prophet might also have been referring to Kennedy's moral imperfections. The young President was a notorious adulterer.

As for going a 'great part of the way', it would be fair to say that Kennedy did achieve a great deal in his short term in office, most notably his championing of civil rights for black Americans, and his determination to end the Cold War.

'Near the river of blood' is widely considered to refer to his brinkmanship during the Cuban Missile Crisis, when he confronted the Soviet Premier, Nikita Khrushchev, and came perilously close to plunging the world into a nuclear war. Alternatively, it may refer to the Red River, not far from Dallas, where Kennedy died.

THE ASSASSINATION

The great man will be struck down in daylight by a thunderbolt.
An evil deed foretold by written petition.
According to the prediction, another falls at night-time.
Conflict at Reims, London and pestilence in Tuscany.

(CENTURY 1 – QUATRAIN 26)

On 22 November 1963, President Kennedy was being driven through Dallas, Texas, in an open-topped car. He and his entourage were in the city to drum up support for the local Democratic Party. Shortly after midday, as the presidential motorcade wound slowly through Dealey Plaza, shots rang out and the back of the President's head was blown away. To the mind's eye of Nostradamus, it must indeed have looked as if he had been struck by a 'thunderbolt'.

As the prophet says in the second line of the quatrain, 'the evil deed was foretold by written petition.' A week before the assassination, Jeanne Dixon, a celebrated Washington psychic, had written to the White House, imploring the President to cancel his visit to Dallas. Sadly, her advice was ignored.

Five years later, Mrs Dixon tried to warn her friend, Senator Robert Kennedy, that his life would be in jeopardy if he visited California. Robert Kennedy was assassinated at 1 a.m. on 5 June, 1968.

The summer of 1968 was the time of student riots in London and Paris, which are referred to in the last line of the quatrain.

THE WITNESS

Before the people, blood will be spilt.
It will not come from the heavens,
But this will not be known for a long time.
The spirit of one person alone shall bear witness to it.

(CENTURY 4 – QUATRAIN 49)

John Kennedy was killed in front of a large crowd which lined the streets of Dallas in the hope of catching a glimpse of the glamorous young President. They saw his blood 'spilt'.

According to the official version, summed up in the massive Warren Commission Report, the President was shot by a lone assassin, Lee Harvey Oswald. The report states that Oswald fired down at the President from the window of a high rise book warehouse on the corner of Dealey Plaza. Countless experts and witnesses have taken issue with this official version of the killing, however, claiming that the fatal shot did not, and could not, have come from the gun of Lee Harvey Oswald. They insist that the angle of penetration proves that the bullet did not come from above – 'did not come from the heavens' – but rather from a grassy knoll at the side of the road.

In the last line of the quatrain, Nostradamus mentions a single witness: could this be the man whose image appeared in a blurry photograph, standing on the knoll at the time of the assassination?

ROBERT KENNEDY

The sudden death of the first person,
Will cause a change and charge another to rule:
Soon, but too late, he achieves a high position at a
young age.
By land and sea he will have been feared.

(CENTURY 4 – QUATRAIN 14)

After the assassination of President Kennedy, the Democratic Party, and the country as a whole, took it as a foregone conclusion that his younger brother, Robert, would eventually take his place. It might well have happened if he, too, had not been gunned down.

On the night of 5 June 1968, Kennedy was at the Ambassador Hotel in Los Angeles. He was in the midst of his Presidential campaign, had just won the California primary, and looked a certainty to win the Democratic nomination for the presidency. Shortly after 1 o'clock he was walking through the hotel kitchen when a young Jordanian, Sirhan Sirhan, stepped out of the shadows and fired several shots at point blank range. Kennedy died twenty-four hours later. He was 43, a 'young age' indeed.

THREE BROTHERS

The Antichrist very soon annihilates all three,
Twenty-seven years his war will last.
The unbelievers are dead, captive, exiled;
With blood, human bodies, water and red hail covering
the earth.

(CENTURY 8 – QUATRAIN 77)

The 'three' in this quatrain are the three Kennedy brothers, John, Robert, and Edward. Much has been made of the fact that only two of the three were assassinated, but in some senses, Edward Kennedy also died, one late night in 1969.

Like his brothers before him, Edward Kennedy had glittering political prospects. At 37, he was the youngest-ever majority whip in the US Senate and was being overtly groomed for the presidency. Then came the Chappaquiddick affair. Kennedy was driving a young woman, Mary Jo Kopechne, home from a party when his car plunged into a river. Kennedy swam to safety, but Mary Jo drowned.

The Senator then proceeded to lie to investigators about the events leading up to the accident. The American public were outraged. What was a married man with eight children doing out at that hour with a young girl in the first place? Why had he not tried to save her? Why had he lied to the authorities? Even the most charitable of his critics accused him of cowardice, not a quality Americans look for in their Presidents. Edward Kennedy's hopes of reaching the White House 'died' there and then.

Nostradamus mentions 'the Antichrist' in the first line of the quatrain. In other prophecies, he states quite clearly that the world will be visited by three Antichrists. It is generally accepted that the first two were Napoleon and Hitler, so was either Oswald or Sirhan Sirhan the third? This is unlikely. What is more probable is that the prophet is using the word Antichrist here in a general way as a force for evil. It could be communism, organised crime or even the CIA, all of which have been blamed for orchestrating the two assassinations.

SPACE

One of President Kennedy's greatest ambitions was to see an American astronaut set foot on the moon, and he became one of the main driving forces behind the space program. His ambition was achieved, but sadly he was no longer alive to witness it. More than four centuries earlier, Nostradamus also predicted that man would one day travel in space, an amazing concept for someone who never witnessed any transport more technically advanced than a horse-drawn carriage.

APOLLO XI

He will travel to the corner of the moon,
Where he will walk on foreign soil.
The unripe fruit will be the subject of great scandal,
Great blame, but also great praise.

(CENTURY 9 – QUATRAIN 65)

The zenith of America's space programme was achieved in July 1969, when Neil Armstrong climbed down from the lunar module of Apollo XI, and became the first human being ever to set foot on the moon. He was indeed walking on the most 'foreign soil' imaginable.

This was, without question, a most astonishing technical achievement, yet, according to Nostradamus, it was destined to become the subject of controversy. There are two possible explanations for the last two lines of this quatrain. One is that, in 1969, America was deeply embroiled in the Vietnam War, and there were those on Capitol Hill who thought the nation's resources would be better spent resolving that particular problem than on space exploration. Erika Cheetham puts forward an alternative explanation. She suggests that the controversy does not apply to the Apollo XI mission at all, but rather to Apollo XIII, whose rockets malfunctioned and left American astronauts temporarily stranded in space. There was 'blame' levelled at NASA for slipshod workmanship, and 'praise' at their ingenuity in engineering the astronauts to safety.

THE CHALLENGER DISASTER

Nine shall be isolated from the rest of humanity,
Isolated from judgment and advice.
Their fate will be sealed from the moment of their departure.
Kappa, Theta, Lambda dead, gone, scattered.

(CENTURY 1 – QUATRAIN 81)

On 28 January 1986, the crew of the 25th Challenger mission were sealed into their craft ready for take-off. Thus far, the Challenger space shuttle program had run virtually flawlessly, and the pre-flight program of this particular mission had run down without any problems. Less than a minute after lift-off, however, Challenger exploded, killing all seven crew members instantly. The tragedy was witnessed by millions around the world on television.

Apart from getting the number of astronauts wrong, Nostradamus describes the situation with remarkable accuracy. It is hard to imagine a situation where one is more 'isolated from humanity' than in the capsule of a space craft. And indeed the fate of the crew of Challenger was 'sealed before their departure.'

THE MIDDLE EAST

Nostradamus showed great interest in the Middle East during the second half of this century. Perhaps this is because he predicted that the third Antichrist would emerge from this region. Some scholars are convinced that he has already emerged in the person of Ayatollah Khomeini or Saddam Hussein. Neither of these candidates for the post really fits the bill, however, because the third Antichrist is supposed to be inextricably linked to the Third World War, which Nostradamus has scheduled for 1999. The Ayatollah is already dead and Saddam Hussein has been effectively neutered by military defeat and subsequent trade sanctions. While both men brought suffering and conflict, neither operated on the scale of the first two Antichrists, Napoleon and Hitler. None the less, Nostradamus's prophecies for this region make fascinating reading.

THE FALL OF THE SHAH

Rain, hunger and conflict without respite in Iran.
Too great a trust will betray the Shah.
The end will begin in France,
A secret omen to the more moderate.

(CENTURY 1 – QUATRAIN 70)

This is the first quatrain in a sequence concerned with Iran and
Iraq, and describes the circumstances leading up to the overthrow
of Shah Muhammad Reza Pahlavi in 1979.

The Shah's troubles dated back to 1953, when he was forced into
exile by the nationalist movement. He returned after a few months,
however, with strong Western support, and developed into a powerful
and progressive ruler, instigating a number of social reforms,
including the emancipation of women. These policies were popular
with one sector of society, but viewed with horror by another, the
Islamic fundamentalists. There was, as Nostradamus said, 'conflict
without respite', and the Shah came to rely increasingly on his secret
police to keep order.

The repressive atmosphere thus created soon
alienated the Shah's erstwhile supporters. By
the early 1970s, he was under attack on both
fronts. Towards the end of the decade, public
discontent with the status quo erupted into
street riots, and the Shah was
forced to impose military
rule. By now he retained his
position of power solely

because of the support he received from America and other Western nations, anxious to protect their oil interests in the region.

Finally, as Nostradamus predicted, his downfall emanated from France. It came in the form of Ayatollah Ruhollah Khomeini, an Islamic holy man, whom the Shah had sent into exile some fifteen years earlier. The Ayatollah had first gone to Iraq and then moved to Paris, from where he conducted his campaign to overthrow the Shah.

THE AYATOLLAH

His hand behind the bloody Alus,
Protection by sea no longer guaranteed.
Between two rivers, the military hand is to be feared.
The black, angry man will make him repent.

(CENTURY 9 – QUATRAIN 33)

One can assume that 'Alus' in the first line of the quatrain is Nostradamus's word for the Shah's brutal secret police, who were, by 1979, his only means of protection against an increasingly hostile population.

'Protection by sea' was 'no longer guaranteed' because the embarrassment caused to his Western supporters by the Shah's increasingly repressive and brutal regime was beginning to outweigh their commercial interests.

'The land between two rivers' – the Tigris and Euphrates – is

Iraq, with whom his country would soon be at war. And 'the black, angry man' is the dark-robed Ayatollah Khomeini, who would soon replace him as head of state.

It was initially a bloodless coup. On 6 January 1979, the Shah lifted military rule, and three days later he went into voluntary exile. The Ayatollah returned to Iran on 1 February to a tumultuous reception and, ten days later, proclaimed the country an Islamic republic.

THE HOSTAGE CRISIS

In 1980, the Shah of Iran will be taken by Egypt.
The months of September and October
Will be a source of great humiliation to the West,
And the beginning of conflict, death and loss.

(CENTURY 3 – QUATRAIN 77)

The Shah left Iran in January 1979 and went to Egypt. From there he roamed the world trying to find a country willing to grant him political asylum. When sanctuary was denied him elsewhere, he returned to Egypt in March 1980. He died in Cairo three months later.

Meanwhile, the Ayatollah set about severing all links with the West and instigated a regime even more repressive and brutal than that of his predecessor. Moderate Iranians, for the most part the better educated, fled Iran in their thousands. Many of them headed to the United States, armed with visas from the American Embassy in Tehran. This exodus threatened Iran's ability to function and on 4 November 1979, in an attempt to stem the flow, the Ayatollah's supporters stormed the embassy and took fifty-three hostages.

The USA responded to this outrage with sanctions and, when they had no effect, the White House sent in a Special Forces unit in an abortive attempt to rescue the hostages. The whole operation was a fiasco, causing the United States untold 'humiliation'.

SADDAM HUSSEIN AND THE GULF WAR

A frightful, wicked and infamous person will enter Iraq
In order to impose his tyranny.
They will all befriend a false republic.
The whole world will be horrified by his hateful face.

(CENTURY 8 – QUATRAIN 70)

By the time the Ayatollah had proclaimed his Islamic republic, another monster had absolute power in Iraq. Saddam Hussein Takriti achieved political power by murdering his political opponents and then his rivals within the Ba'ath Party. He is graphically described in this quatrain by Nostradamus.

In 1980, war broke out between Iraq and Iran. It wore on for eight years, during which time Iraq received billions of dollars in aid from the West, together with naval support to enable it to keep the Gulf open for shipping. In 1990, Saddam repaid this generosity by demanding thirty billion dollars from Saudi Arabia, with threats of aggression if the demand were not met.

OPERATION DESERT STORM

The Europeans will come:
Americans accompanied by the British and others.
They will lead a great military force, coloured and white,
And go against the leader of Iraq.

(CENTURY 10 – QUATRAIN 86)

On 1 August 1990, Saddam Hussein invaded and occupied Kuwait. A week later, American and British forces started to assemble in Saudi Arabia in preparation for a counter-attack. Eventually, forces from twelve nations joined the joint operation, 'coloured and white'.

Saddam boasted that he would unleash 'a holocaust' against the alliance in the 'mother of all battles'. In actuality, the war lasted a mere seven days, during which time Saddam's army was routed.

CHAPTER 10

INTO THE NEXT MILLENNIUM

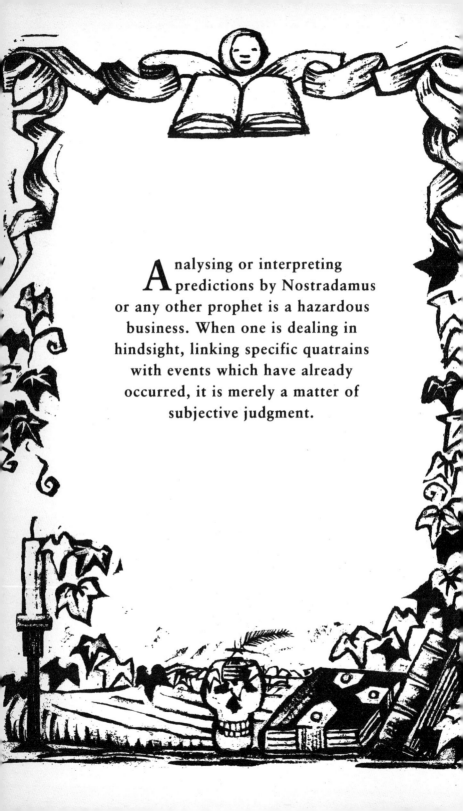

Analysing or interpreting predictions by Nostradamus or any other prophet is a hazardous business. When one is dealing in hindsight, linking specific quatrains with events which have already occurred, it is merely a matter of subjective judgment.

When attempting to predict the future by interpreting the prophecies, however, one is on much stickier ground. Even accepting that Nostradamus was a prophet of great genius, the very nature of his quatrains – their complexity and ambiguity – makes it virtually impossible to unscramble what he foresaw for our future.

That said, there are a number of themes, most of them pessimistic, which recur through the *Centuries* and can only be seen as relating to events yet to come. These include the coming of 'Mabus', the third Antichrist; nuclear war in Europe and America; world domination by the East; countless natural disasters; the demise of the Roman Catholic church; and the arrival on earth of extraterrestrial beings. This section of the book looks at a handful of quatrains and attempts to link them with events which may or may not happen. It is, therefore, one writer's shot in the dark. This is very much a DIY section, and the reader should actively question the conclusions presented and feel free to reinterpret the lines in any way he or she feels fit.

NATURAL DISASTERS

AIDS

To the port of Agde, the ships will enter,
Carrying the infection of the pestilence, not the faith.
Passing the bridge, a thousand thousand will be taken.
And the bridge broken by the resistance of the third one.

(CENTURY 8 – QUATRAIN 21)

The is no clue to the date of this particular prediction, but it is one of several which is generally considered to refer to the current epidemic of AIDS. Scientists investigating the virus have traced its origins back to central Africa where it existed in the monkey population as far back as 1945. It is thought to have passed to the human population by a person or persons having been bitten by the infected monkeys. The disease was then carried to the USA and thence to Europe by migrant workers, most of whom would have travelled from their native country by 'ship'.

Nostradamus mentions a 'thousand thousand' being taken. Tragically this would appear to be a gross underestimate. Figures published by Harvard University calculate that, if a cure has not been found, there will by 100 million adults and 10 million children infected with the HIV virus by the end of the century. It is not surprising, therefore, that many experts on Nostradamus now think that we need look no further than this epidemic for the prophet's vision of the apocalypse.

> **When the sacred temples have been plundered,**
> **The greatest of lands profaning holy things.**
> **Because of their actions, an enormous pestilence will arrive.**
> **The King will not condemn them for their actions.**

(CENTURY 8 – QUATRAIN 62)

As we have seen throughout the *Centuries*, Nostradamus was firmly convinced that all plagues and natural disasters were the result of divine retribution. AIDS would, in his mind, be the ultimate proof of this view. In the West, it was originally passed almost exclusively within the homosexual and drug-using cultures, lifestyles which the prophet would certainly have deemed as offensive in the sight of the Almighty. In the last line of the quatrain, however, Nostradamus also suggests that, having been punished for their deeds, the sinners will ultimately be forgiven in accordance with Christian teaching.

So great a famine from the wave of pestilence,
That rains a long time the length of the Arctic pole.
Samarobrin is a hundred leagues from the hemisphere.
They will live without law, exempt from politics.

(CENTURY 6 – QUATRAIN 5)

This is yet another quatrain which is widely considered to refer to the AIDS epidemic. What precisely Nostradamus is actually getting at is somewhat more controversial, however. Among the more plausible interpretations is that of J H Brennan, who suggests that the epidemic will become so widespread that huge colonies will be established to isolate the victims of the virus. It seems a bit harsh and improbable that they would be consigned to the polar regions, but man has done worse things in the past. There is little doubt that any victim subjected to such a fate would 'live without law' and would be 'exempt from politics'. Another suggestion is that the quatrain is in fact describing a future cure for the virus, perhaps a vaccine produced at very low temperatures. If the researcher who eventually achieves this miracle is a reader of Nostradamus, he might well be tempted to call it Samarobrin.

> When those of the North Pole are assembled,
> In the east there will be great fear and trembling.
> A new man will be elected, sustained by great fear.
> Rhodes and Byzantium stained by un-Christian blood.

(CENTURY 6 – QUATRAIN 31)

Again in this quatrain, Nostradamus seems to be suggesting some connection between the polar regions and the AIDS epidemic. And again some interpreters consider this a reinforcement for the theory of a quarantine zone in the Arctic or Antarctic. What is certain is that the prophet foresees the global spread of the virus by 'un-Christian' blood.

GLOBAL WARMING

> At a latitude of forty-eight degrees,
> At the end of Cancer, there is a very great drought.
> Fish in the seas, rivers and lakes will be boiled.
> Bearn and Biggore in distress and from the sky, fire.

(CENTURY 5 – QUATRAIN 98)

Nostradamus gives us a date – Cancer ends on July 22 – but not a year for this prediction. Several interpreters of Nostradamus agree on the significance of the third line of this quatrain, which sets it apart from the other prophecies of drought. The image of fish boiling in the lakes and rivers suggests an increase in temperature so severe that they can no longer support marine life.

Populated lands will become uninhabitable.
Over fields there will be great disagreement.
Kingdoms will be given over to those without prudence.
The great forces, death and dissension.

(CENTURY 2 – QUATRAIN 95)

This quatrain is sometimes linked to the apocalypse, but it is more plausible as a prediction of the catastrophic effects of the erosion of the earth's ozone layer and the consequent global warming. If indeed this occurs, 'populated lands' would certainly become 'uninhabitable', and the social and political chaos this would cause would create 'great disagreement'.

WORLD FAMINE

The great famine which will visit the earth,
Will be spasmodic and then become universal.
It will be so complete and long lasting that people
will harvest
Roots from the woods and the child from the breast.

(CENTURY 1 – QUATRAIN 67)

In this quatrain, Nostradamus seems to be suggesting that, at some unspecified time in the future, famine will spread from the Third World and will afflict the entire globe. The idea that people will be obliged to eat roots, and cannibalize their own children, suggests a total breakdown of world agriculture. The only possible reasons for that happening are either a nuclear holocaust or a radical change in the earth's atmosphere.

The year that Saturn and Mars are equally bright,
The air is terribly dry with a great meteor.
Because of this secret fire, a great place burns in the sun.
There will be little rain, warm winds, war and incursions.

(CENTURY 4 – QUATRAIN 67)

The first line of this quatrain is an astrological clue to the date and, if the prediction applies to the immediate future, it suggests March 1996. The actual prediction again suggest the devastating effects of global warming – 'the air is terribly dry ... a great place burns in the sun.'

EARTHQUAKE IN INDIA AND THE NEAR EAST

Mars, Mercury and the Moon in conjunction.
Towards the south there will be a great drought.
An earthquake will be reported from the bottom of India.
Greece and Asia Minor will also be affected.

(CENTURY 3 – QUATRAIN 3)

The astrological references in the first line of this quatrain offer us several possible dates for the coming catastrophe. They are December 1995, March or June 1996, March 1998 and July-August in the year 2000.

EARTHQUAKE IN AMERICA

When the sun is in twenty degrees of Taurus, there will be a
terrible earthquake.
The great city full of people will be shattered.
The air, heaven and Earth will be shrouded in darkness,
When the infidel ignores God and the Saints.

(CENTURY 9 – QUATRAIN 83)

Here again Nostradamus gives us an exact date – 10 May – for a natural disaster, but declines to mention a year. The most likely victims – 'great cities' – of a massive 'quake would appear to be either Los Angeles or San Francisco, both of which lie on the San Andreas fault. The last line of the quatrain is ambiguous, however. The 'infidel' could refer to a people who had turned away from God, which to a great extent would cover the population of California. On the other hand, it could refer to a people who did not practice Christianity in the first place. If this is accurate, the most likely candidate for the cataclysm would appear to be Tokyo or one of the other great Japanese cities.

VOLCANIC ERUPTION

Earth shaking and fire from the centre of the earth
Will cause the towers of the New City to shake.
Two great rocks will war for a long time
And Arethusa will cover the new river red.

(CENTURY 1 – QUATRAIN 87)

This quatrain clearly predicts an eruption of one of the world's major volcanoes, an event which will be followed by an earthquake. The two 'great rocks' might well refer to the Earth's continental plates, which constantly grind against one another.

The volcano mentioned here could, of course, be Etna, Mont Pelée or Vesuvius, but this author tends to favour Mount Rainier in Washington State. If it were to erupt, it could easily inundate the 'new city' of Tacoma, and its effects would be felt as far away as the state capital, Seattle.

CATASTROPHE IN CORNWALL

The ground trembles at Mortara,
Cornwall of St George half sunk.
By peace made drowsy, war erupts.
In the church at Easter, the abyss opens.

(CENTURY 9 – QUATRAIN 31)

This quatrain predicts some terrible natural catastrophe which will cause Cornwall to be submerged. Many people have interpreted it as an earthquake, followed by a tidal wave and, while this is possible, one must consider, in light of recent meteorological revelations, that Nostradamus may be referring to global warming and the rise in sea level, resulting from the melting of the polar regions.

EXTRATERRESTRIALS

**Near Auch, Lectoure and Mirande,
A great fire from heaven for three nights will fall.
The cause will be seen as both amazing and miraculous.
Afterwards the earth will tremble.**

(CENTURY 1 – QUATRAIN 46)

Nostradamus wrote a number of quatrains which have been widely interpreted as predicting a visit to earth by beings from another planet. As J H Brennan points out in his book, *Nostradamus – Visions of the Future*, this apparently outrageous suggestion is inherently feasible. 'While we now know for certain that earth is the only planet to support intelligent life, the probability of life elsewhere in the universe is a statistical certainty.

'Given this, scientific objections to theories of extraterrestrial visitations are generally based on the enormous distances which would have to be travelled, even from the nearest star. Since the speed of light represents the absolute upper limit of velocity of any physical craft, interstellar travel would have to measured in terms of years, hundreds, even thousands of years. What sort of being, the sceptics ask, would waste that amount of time to visit a backward planet of an obscure solar system on the edge of a mediocre galaxy. The answer is, of course, one that lives a great deal longer than we do.'

If such a space craft were to land on earth, it might well look like a 'great fire from heaven'; it would certainly be viewed as 'amazing and miraculous'.

Nostradamus gives us no idea when this event might occur, but other quatrains dealing with alien landings tend to suggest, via astrological clues, that the time frame lies somewhere within the next ten years.

The gods will arrive in the guise of humans,
And they will be the cause of great conflict.
Before, the sky was seen to be free of arms.
The greatest damage will be caused in the west.

(CENTURY 1 – QUATRAIN 91)

This quatrain again suggest a visitation by aliens – 'Gods who arrive in the guise of humans'. The 'conflict' they will cause would probably take the form of mass panic, much like that triggered by Orson Welles's infamous broadcast of *War of the Worlds*.

The fact that the sky is 'free of arms' suggests that the arrival is destined for the early part of the next century, after World War III and during the millennium of peace which Nostradamus promises will follow.

THE COLLAPSE OF CHRISTIANITY

From North Africa, the reign will reach to Europe.
Fire the city and cut without pity.
The great one of Asia will come by land and sea with
multitudes.
The cross will be devalued and driven out.

(CENTURY 6 – QUATRAIN 80)

Again, Nostradamus gives us no specific timeframe for this quatrain, but he seems to be suggesting not only the spread of Islamic fundamentalism, but the actual demise of the Christian religion – 'the cross'.

THE APOCALYPSE 1999?

In the year 1999, and seven months after,
From the sky will come the great King of Terror.
Resuscitating the great king of the Mongols,
Before which Mars will reign in peace.

(CENTURY 9 – QUATRAIN 72)

This particular quatrain has given rise to considerable controversy and has been interpreted in numerous ways. To many students of

Nostradamus, it is the ultimate of his apocalyptic prophecies and foretells the end of the world in 1999. Consistent with this interpretation, the 'great King of Terror', is thought to be Mabus, the third Antichrist. The idea that he 'comes from the sky' could either suggest that Mabus is some sort of extraterrestrial being or, more plausibly, that he will launch his attacks from the sky, probably in the form of nuclear missiles. Many scholars consider that the mention of him 'resuscitating the Great King of the Moguls' suggests that the third Antichrist will emanate from the middle or far East and will live in the spirit of the great warrior king, Genghis Kahn.

OR LATER?

After the moon has reigned for twenty years,
Another will assume his seven thousand year reign;
When the sun shall take up his days,
Then my prophecy will be accomplished.

(CENTURY 1 – QUATRAIN 48)

In this quatrain, Nostradamus seems to be confirming a notion commonly held in the Middle Ages, that the world would end at the beginning of the seventh millennium. This flies directly in the face of the prophecy which gives 1999 as the year of the apocalypse. Or does it? James Laver comes up with an intriguing explanation for the apparent discrepancy. It is his belief that the seven millennium theory came from the pre-Christian *Book of Enoch*, a document with which Nostradamus would no doubt have been familiar.

It appears that in his calculations the prophet counted backwards 4000 years before the birth of Christ, took this as his starting point, and then simply added two thousand years, bringing us up to the start of the seventh millennium, the year 2001.

THE SEVENTH MILLENNIUM

When the wheel of time has reached the seventh millennium,
There will begin games of death,
Not long from the age of the thousand years,
When those who have entered the tomb shall emerge from it.

(CENTURY 10 – QUATRAIN 74)

Again in this quatrain, Nostradamus seems to be suggesting that the world will face some sort of catastrophe at the beginning of the seventh millennium but, as Laver suggests above, this might well not refer to 6001 AD but, because of retrospective timing to the perceived date of the Creation, it could just as well mean the year 2001.

All is not doom and gloom in this particular quatrain, however. The last line suggests that after a thousand years 'those who have entered the tomb shall emerge from it.' The 'tomb' could well be interpreted as a fall-out shelter and, if this is the case, Nostradamus is predicting that, in the aftermath of a nuclear holocaust, there will be survivors who will able to emerge into the world when radiation levels fall.

MABUS

It is generally accepted that Mabus – a corruption of the Latin 'Malus', meaning the Evil one – who is mentioned in several quatrains, is the third Antichrist of Nostradamus. There is a general consensus upon the identity of the first two – Napoleon and Hitler – but there is wide disagreement about the identity of Mabus. It appears clear that, whoever he might be, he will emanate from the east. Some scholars think he is already here in the person of Saddam Hussein or Colonel Gaddafi. Others have suggested that he might not even be a national leader, but an individual terrorist who single-handedly sparks the war. This is not such a stupid notion when one considers the actions of the young student, Gavrilo Princip, who, by assassinating Arch-Duke Franz Ferdinand of Austria in Sarajevo in 1914, plunged the world into World War I.

A third school of thought is that Mabus is not a person at all, but a whole nation. China, for instance, with its colossal population, already has nuclear capability. Whoever or whatever Mabus may be, it is worth examining a few quatrains which throw some light onto the subject.

From beyond Russia and the Black Sea,
There will be a leader who will come to France.
He will pass through Alanica and America,
And will leave his bloody lance in Byzantium.

(CENTURY 5 – QUATRAIN 54)

Like so many of the quatrains looking into the distant future, these lines are cryptic in the extreme. They seem to be suggesting that a great leader will emerge from the East and gradually make his way through Western Europe and into the Americas.

Long awaited, he will never return in Europe,
But he shall appear in Asia.
One of the league issues from the great Hermes,
He will grow above all other powers in the Orient.

(CENTURY 10 – QUATRAIN 75)

In this quatrain, Nostradamus merely serves to reinforce his belief that the third Antichrist will eventually arise in Asia.

Mabus will soon die, then there will be
Terrible slaughter of the people and animals.
Suddenly, vengeance shall be revealed.
A hundred to hand, thirst and hunger when the comet will pass.

(CENTURY 2 – QUATRAIN 62)

This quatrain suggests that Mabus will not live to see the results of his handiwork, but they will be terrible indeed. The 'terrible slaughter of people and animals' suggests nuclear war. The mention of the comet passing could refer to Halley's comet, which is next due in 2062, or it could be describing ballistic missiles delivering nuclear bombs.

RISE OF THE EAST

Sooner or later you will see great changes made.
Extreme horrors and vengeance.
As Islam is thus led by its angel,
The heavens draw near to the balance.

(CENTURY 1 – QUATRAIN 56)

Here Nostradamus suggests a massive conflict between East and West. He frequently used the word 'balance' to denote democracy and 'Islam' is, of course, a generic to denote all the powers of the Middle East.

248

NUCLEAR TERRORISM

**From the East there will be unleashed a terrible act,
Which will strike at the Adriatic sea and the heirs of
Romulus.
With the Libyan fleet, the inhabitants of Malta,
And its archipelago will tremble with fear.**

(CENTURY 1 – QUATRAIN 9)

Again, Nostradamus reasserts his belief that World War III will by initiated by the powers of the East. This particular quatrain could be describing an isolated action in such a war, or it could be describing an act of nuclear terrorism. It suggests quite clearly that an attack will be launched against Malta and Italy – 'the heirs of Romulus' – probably by a nuclear device launched from a ship, or more likely a submarine.

WORLD WAR III

After mankind's greatest misery, an even greater approaches.
The cycle of the centuries is renewed:
It will rain blood, milk, famine, war and disease.
In the sky there will be seen a fire, dragging a trail of sparks.

(CENTURY 2 – QUATRAIN 46)

One assumes that Nostradamus uses 'mankind's greatest misery' to describe the horrors of World War II. If this is the case, then one has a dreadful suspicion that the 'even greater' one will be World War III.

Opinion is sharply divided on the second line of the quatrain. 'The cycle of the centuries renewed' could well denote the end of this millennium. An equally strong argument can be put forward, however, that Nostradamus could have been referring to the end of any millennium in the future.

The prophet's nightmare scenario for the ultimate nuclear war is accurate in many ways. The number of people killed by the blast of the bombs will be far outweighed by those who linger on, only to fall victim to radiation poisoning or to starvation. His 'rain of blood' could well describe the torrential downpour which usually follows a nuclear explosion and the rain itself would be clogged with radioactive particles.

The last line could be describing the rockets

used to deliver the nuclear devices, or it could refer to Halley's Comet, which is a popular dating mechanism used by Nostradamus. If the latter is true, then the next possible date for World War Three would fall in 2062 when the comet next returns.

NUCLEAR ATTACK ON PARIS

There will be let loose living fire and hidden death,
Horror inside dreadful globes.
By night, Paris will be reduced to dust.
The city on fire will be helpful to the enemy.

(CENTURY 5 – QUATRAIN 8)

The meaning of this quatrain could not be more straightforward. The 'living fire' in the first line is the nuclear explosion itself; 'the hidden death' is the radioactive fall out which follows. Nostradamus describes 'horror inside dreadful globes' which could either describe bombs or nuclear warheads. It is obvious that the target of this particular attack is Paris, but the prophet gives us no clue as to when this might happen.

NUCLEAR ATTACK ON NEW YORK

Forty-five degrees the sky will burn.
Fire engulfs the great new city.
Immediately, huge, scattered flames will shoot heavenward,
When they wish to see the Normans proven.

(CENTURY 6 – QUATRAIN 97)

There is, of course, an element of guesswork when attributing a precise location of 'the great new city.' but most interpreters of the quatrains agree that it is most probably New York City, which lies between the 40th and 45th parallels. Other writers argue that the mention of 'Normans' in the last line places the attack in Paris, though it would be hard, even in Nostradamus's day, to describe the French capital as a 'new' city.

THE AFTERMATH

The garden of the world, near the new city,
In the road of the hollow mountains.
It will be seized and plunged into the tank,
Forced to drink water poisoned with sulphur.

(CENTURY 10 – QUATRAIN 49)

Here again Nostradamus refers to the 'new city', and once again one is tempted to assume he is referring to New York. In fact, this quatrain dovetails into the previous one. 'Road of hollow mountains' describes the city's towering skyscrapers quite neatly. And, in the aftermath of a nuclear holocaust, the water supply would inevitably be contaminated, not with sulphur, but with radioactive particles.

Erika Cheetham puts forward an intriguing alternative interpretation to this quatrain. She suggests that it refers to the meltdown of a nuclear reactor at Three Mile Island in 1979. The reactor was located at Harrisburg, Pennsylvania, which lies less than 180 miles from New York City. It has long been suspected that there has been under-ground leakage of nuclear waste from the reactor and that this might, in time, affect the water table.

THE END OF THE WORLD

The world is close to its last days.
Saturn will again be slow to return.
The empire moves towards the Brodde Nation.
The eye plucked from Narbonne by a goshawk.

(CENTURY 3 – QUATRAIN 92)

This is one of the very few quatrains in which Nostradamus specifically refers to the end of the world. For reasons that have been stated elsewhere in this chapter, it is extremely unlikely that he is calculating this to happen in the year 2000 or before. J H Brennan makes an interesting argument to back up this belief. Nostradamus mentions Narbonne, a ancient city in south-east France, a place which is still very much on the map. In the previous line, however, he mentions the 'Brodde Nation', which to the best of my knowledge is yet to exist. It is, therefore, extremely unlikely for an entirely new and powerful world force to emerge in the space of five years. The date for the apocalypse must be some time much further ahead in history.